Nine Challenges for Parents

NINE CHALLENGES for PARENTS

Leading Your Child into
Responsible Adulthood

Lucy & William Hulme

Augsburg
MINNEAPOLIS

NINE CHALLENGES FOR PARENTS
Leading Your Child into Responsible Adulthood

Interior design: Peregrine Publications
Cover design: Koechel-Peterson Design

Library of Congress Cataloging-in-Publication Data

Hulme, Lucy
    Nine challenges for parents: leading your child into responsible adulthood /
    Lucy and William Hulme.
        p. cm.
    ISBN 0-8066-2657-7
        1. Childrearing—Religious aspects—Christianity. I. Hulme, William
    Edward, 1920–   II. Title.
    HQ769.3.H85   1993
    649'.1—dc20   93–24244
                                                              CIP

The paper used in this publication meets the minimum requirements of American National Standard for Information Sciences—Permanence of Paper for Printed Library Materials, ANSI Z329.48–1984.   ∞™

Manufactured in the U.S.A.   AF 9–2657
97   96   95   94   93   1   2   3   4   5   6   7   8   9   10

▼

Contents

5

▼▼

Preface

▲▲

It takes a bit of audacity to write a book about parenting. Being a parent oneself is all one needs to understand how audacious it is. We are not experts. We have read and listened to the experts and profited from them—authorities as diverse as Thomas Gordon, John Rosemond, and James Dobson—and find them all valuable. Though our children are now adults, we are still in the process of being parents. From what we can ascertain at this point in life, the process will never end this side of death.

Who in a moment of a parenting crisis would consider themselves experts? At these critical moments we parents seem to be far more aware of our shortcomings than our children perhaps realize. Some of us may be like the mother who would insist she was right when she was with her children, but in her lonely moments she would burst into tears and cry out, "I'm such a failure!" Others of us may tell our children how inadequate we feel. The authors are no exception to experiencing the ups and downs of parenting. There are many pains as well as joys in our memories.

So why are we writing this book? Because we have a resource for parenting in our biblical heritage, and we believe we have an understanding of this resource. That heritage has been most helpful to us, and we believe we can illustrate how it can be helpful to other parents. We are people of faith and this faith has content, which is known as the Word of God. But our faith is more than content since the Word of God is a living Word. It communicates the living God who inspires us with hope. In the midst of our parental frustrations, we are aware that a power beyond our own is still there when our parenting functioning seems to be floundering.

We live in a competitive world, a world of comparisons, even in parenting. When parents get together, what do they talk about? Their children, of course, and often they tell only the good things they are accomplishing. Other parents may be left wondering whether their children are doing as well. This game that parents tend to play is called PTA in transactional analysis. It is also often played in annual Christmas letters.

▼

We hope that, by seeing their parenthood within the biblical heritage, parents will be in a good position to maintain the values and priorities of their faith from the beginning.

Our culture tends to lay guilt trips on parents, but guilt by itself only makes us less effective and less spontaneous as parents. We need something that can turn this guilt into something positive. Our biblical heritage has that something in the great good news of God's forgiving love.

Some people are simply naturals at being parents. What can we offer them? In this book we can offer them biblical affirmation of their parenting and help them to deepen their appreciation of God, their own nurturing Heavenly Parent. Others—the majority—have to work at parenting. What comes naturally to them may not be an asset to their parenting. To those parents we hope to offer new insights into their relationship to their children as well as to their parents. They may also receive the vision of hope in their calling as parents, and through this vision, the power to act on the insights that they have received. This book is also for those who are expecting their first child. We hope that, by seeing their parenthood within the biblical heritage, they will be in a good position to maintain the values and priorities of their faith from the beginning.

But this book is also for parents of children of all ages— toddlers, children, adolescents, and young adults. We believe it will help you better to understand the uniqueness of your child and to release your best in parenting.

We have reared five children—three girls and two boys— and are now grandparents, a fascinating experience in itself. For several years we have conducted parenting workshops in family camps and in churches. From these experiences and the good feedback and satisfaction we have received from them came the desire to write this book.

▼▼▼

Preparing Children to Leave

▲▲▲

The goal of parenting is the development of maturity that permits children to leave their father and mother. During the long dependency period of childhood, parents need to be aware of obstacles that hinder their children's leaving process. Among them are unmet needs from the parents' own childhoods, inadequate teaching of self-discipline and responsibility, and the conditioning we all receive from the values and priorities of our culture.

Leaving Home

While working in our flower garden recently, I (Bill) bumped against the trunk of a small tree and immediately heard a fluttering. Looking up, I saw a small dove fly to the ground and flutter along the ground away from me. Thinking it could not yet fly, I was concerned about whether it would escape the predatory nature of our cat. Then another dove flew from the tree to the fluttering bird and began to "dialogue" physically with it, doing what looked like a dance. Both birds took off, flying high enough to clear our neighbor's fence. Then I realized that the second dove was the mother. The smaller dove could fly but needed the mother's encouragement, instruction, or whatever was happening in that dance. The mother knew this and rescued her small one from its potentially fatal predicament.

What birds do by instinct, humans accomplish by decision making. Yet we say we have a parental instinct. But it does not appear to be equally distributed throughout the species. We will take a look at the factors that play a role in our decision making as parents.

As parents you may be assisting your child to take his or her first steps (or you can recall when you did so), not unlike the mother dove assisting the young dove. But there the similarity ends. The young dove was learning to fly and would soon leave its mother. After that, it would have to take care of itself, get its own food, and protect itself against predators. When a child learns to walk, it means just the opposite. Rather than leaving his or her parents, the child who has just learned to walk needs more, not less, parental care to prevent its walking into danger.

▼

The process whereby children leave their parents begins long before they actually leave. It began when they left their mother's womb.

The process whereby children leave their parents begins long before they actually leave. In fact, it began when they left their mother's womb where all of their needs were met. Never again, no matter how capable their parents, will their needs be so completely met. So leaving the womb is a foreshadowing of leaving home.

For human beings, leaving home is a gradual process that takes years to accomplish. The process can run into snags that can complicate and delay it. Yet the process itself is as necessary for humans as it is for birds. A familiar Bible verse, probably read at your wedding, describes the leaving process: "Therefore a man leaves his father and his mother and clings to his wife, and they become one flesh" (Gen. 2:24). While this verse pictures marriage as the culmination of leaving, it is actually describing the process of becoming adult—of accepting the responsibilities of adulthood, one of which may be marriage. Looking at the culmination process, we can conclude that marriage is not for children but for adults.

We cannot tell what goes on in the minds of mother bird and little bird when the leaving process is upon them. In their instinctively governed world, they may be spared the pain of leaving that human parents and children may experience. But we can easily imagine the baby bird's anxiety as the mother flew to its rescue.

Even as the process of leaving father and mother to assume adult responsibilities does not begin around the ages of eighteen to twenty-one, it may not be completed by then either. In fact, leaving our childhood homes is a lifelong process into which we seem to gain more and more insight as we go from one stage of living to another.

Among the illusions we hold about the leaving process is the belief that if you move out of your parental home to establish your own, you have left father and mother. You *may* have, but you may *not* have, depending on how free you are from your parents whom by now you have internalized in your mind.

Both my (Bill's) maternal and paternal grandparents left home in their late teens or early adulthood never to return. Their parents never were able to visit them. All came from Europe, and in those days leaving for America meant that in all likelihood they would never see their parents again. One wonders what effect such complete separation had on the leaving process. While we do not know the answer, we can be sure that it was not always as clean a break as the one-way passage might indicate.

Others have strongly rebelled against their parents and left, never desiring to return. One young man was so angry and hurt over the bitterness of his parents' divorce that he broke all ties with them. None of his family even knows where he is. Obviously he left home in a most radical way, but whether he was able to leave emotionally is another question. We might suspect that his rebellious anger complicated rather than facilitated the emotional leaving. How, for example, is he relating to his internalized parents from whom he cannot run away?

Theologian Henri Nouwen describes the role of parenting as being a host to one's children.[1] The "host" knows that the "guest" will eventually leave, and the host's task is to provide hospitality while the guest is present. This is a detached view of parenting. I doubt if Nouwen could have come up with it were he actually a parent. This, however, does not mean that he is not in some ways correct. But it is difficult to turn this insight into a functioning principle while faced with the demanding challenges of being a parent.

When you stand back from a picture, for example, you often get a different perspective than when you stand up close to it. So when you are up close to the parenting process, it is difficult for the parental host to resist the influences that make the guest's leaving difficult. Once these influences take hold on us—and I do not know that they can be fully avoided—the parental host becomes so heavily invested in the children guests that the analogy no longer holds. Psychoanalyst Ann Miller[2] says that rather than leaving our childhood homes, we can actually become prisoners of them. How can we leave and become adult if we are a prisoner to our own childhood? And the parent can become as bound to the past as the child.

Some societies have processes for leaving father and mother. For example, in years past, some Native Americans had rites of passage for their adolescent boys and girls. The boys in particular were exposed to hardships in the wild where they had to cope on their own to survive. We technological-age parents are more likely to protect our children from such dangers or to rescue them if they were so endangered. Yet our culture actually can be more harsh toward our children than that of the Native Americans. We send our young people to fight dangerous wars in trouble spots around the world. In these dangerous conflicts, they experience violence far more severe than the Native Americans' rites of passage. In those societies the youth were at least supported in their ordeals by the security of tradition and the solidarity of their social system.

Despite the developmental differences between birds and humans, the parental task in both species is the same. Teaching the young to fly means teaching them to be responsible: to get their own food, to protect themselves, to develop their own resources for coping with their environment, and to establish their own families. Groups of people who have lived close to nature like the birds have developed their own culturally approved ways of teaching their young to leave. We who consider ourselves advanced have lost much of this social solidarity and are vulnerable to all the problems that arise when we have to make decisions on our own.

Recognizing Holdovers
from Our Childhood Home

When we have to make decisions on our own, we are probably drawing on memories from our childhood homes. While we may react instinctively in these moments, our instincts may not be as wise as those of the birds. So we parents need to ask ourselves what we may be carrying with us that we should have left behind when we left our fathers and mothers.

You can usually tell what these dated reactive patterns are by recalling the times when you have reacted impulsively or rigidly, or acted with some anger rather than logic in dealing with your children. Is this a pattern that you have repeated many times? If so, you are probably following a script that was imprinted on your mind during your childhood. Reflect on that script. Do you recall incidents in your own childhood from which you might have picked it up? Then you were on the child end of it; now you have taken over the parent end.

▼

When we have to make decisions on our own, we are probably drawing on memories from our childhood homes.

Reflect on your childhood home as you focus on your present family situation. Ask yourself, for example, what you as a child thought you really needed to have. This is the area where you may likely "push" your children. You of course will have good rational reasons for your pushing, but basically it is rooted in unfinished business from your own childhood.

For example, I (Bill) thought it was important to have friends throughout childhood and adolescence. I probably picked this up from my parents, realizing that they wanted me to have friends, particularly from families that they respected. Although I had friends, I never felt I had them in abundance. So without my resolving this baggage from my childhood, I proceeded to project my anxieties about having friends onto my children and impulsively pushed them toward other children. If their efforts did not work out,

I felt the same old anxieties I felt as a child. Because I could not dispassionately talk to them about my anxiety, I projected my own childhood shame onto them. We need to identify areas in which our unfinished needs interfere with our children's ability to live their own lives and grow toward maturity.

Discipline: Laying a Foundation for Maturity

Self-discipline is essential for maturity. It is an asset that enables our children to be able to take charge of themselves, leave their childhood home, and direct their lives according to their beliefs and values. Undisciplined people are swayed by many opinions and suggestions; they cannot seem to accomplish much.

Charles de Gaulle is supposed to have said, "Only the disciplined are free." If we lack the fundamental structure of discipline, we will find it hard to function well with others and may have difficulty reaching our goals. The self-disciplined have an internal referent and are able to direct themselves. They accept the necessary structures essential for an orderly society, yet they can think for themselves. Thus they are able both to exhibit self-control and to show concern for others.

For our children's sake, we ourselves need to be mature and self-disciplined. They will become more self-confident when we show that we know where we want firmness. Children do not want us to overidentify with them but want us to connect with their need to become adults. The best way a child can know how to be adult is to be with *real* adults.

The word discipline comes from the same root word as disciple, and both refer to learning. A disciple is a learner, and discipline is putting learning into practice. We are our children's teachers.

Parents have to realize that they can't be liked by their children every minute of the day. As we try to direct our children's actions or inhibit or change some behaviors, we can expect resistance. Yet without discipline, family life would be chaos. As children learn the rules and see that they are consistently and positively enforced, they begin to internalize them and feel comfortable with them. "In our house, we always wash our hands before we eat," one child told her visiting friend. "No, I can't go to a movie on a week night, but how about Friday or Saturday?" said another.

A large task for us as parents is not only to discipline (teach) our children, but also to help them internalize a sense of order. If a child reaches school age without basic training in democratic living, the school will have to start at the beginning to teach discipline and responsibility, a task it is often not well equipped to do.

In spite of the benefits of constructive discipline, our children will likely still resist our efforts. Their own desires lead them to reject much of what we suggest, even when our messages are clear and the children would benefit by following our guidance. The process of teaching our children how to live well requires continuous creativity.

A wise friend gave an example of such a fresh approach when she heard the screech of brakes in front of her home one day. Going out to investigate, she found several children enjoying the excitement of a dangerous game. They would send one of their number to run in front of an oncoming car and then quickly return to the curb.

Our friend knew that if she yelled at them to stop, they would probably go elsewhere and continue their "fun." Instead she walked up to them as they concentrated on their game and asked, "What are you planning to do when one of you is all bloody with a broken leg?"

Startled, the children did not answer.

"Well," she said, "you'd better make a plan. Who is going to ring the doorbell and ask for help? Have you ever seen someone hit by a car?" Finally, one of them said, "I guess we never thought of that," and the group dispersed. Her creative approach had been a great teacher. The children did not feel justified in continuing their destructive behavior, because they were helped to see beyond their "fun."

By giving our children workable tasks, such as preparing for bed at a certain time or setting or clearing the table, we lay the foundation for the future. Responsibility comes from experiencing the result of their doing or not doing everyday tasks. A key in discipline is helping children see the direct result of their neglect. Having to wear a soiled T-shirt again and hearing a sibling complain about the lack of clothes make it clear to a child that he or she forgot to do the laundry.

Resisting Cultural Pressures

The goal of parenting is to help our children develop the maturity needed to leave father and mother. A major obstacle preventing maturity is the conditioning we receive from our culture.

As parents we find ourselves under pressure to shape our children according to cultural expectations of what they should be. This delays the normal maturation process. As Christians we experience a tension with the values and priorities of our culture. This is simply our particular culture's version of the Christian conflict with the world. It is built into our calling. We are *in* the world but not *of* it. This conflict is clearly expressed in Jesus' prayer for his followers shortly before he was crucified: "They are not of the world, even as I am not of it. Sanctify them by the truth; your word is truth. As you have sent me into the world, I have sent them into the world" (John 17:16-18 NIV).

▼

The problem is that we have the world within us as well as outside us, meaning that we have an inner affinity for the world as well as an inner resistance to it.

Being *in* but not *of* our world, we experience a difficult tension within which to rear children. It has always been so. Some early Christians found it difficult to live in their society and left to live in the deserts, apart from the world. Some banded together and formed monasteries and convents. In later centuries whole groups of families decided to withdraw, such as the Mennonites, the Amish, and similar groups. But the separation has never been total. They always took some of the surrounding culture with them. Their community conflicts often resemble the conflicts experienced outside their communities. The Amish in the upper midwest, for example, were in bitter conflict among themselves over whether or not they could obey the law requiring colored reflectors on their buggies. Some said it was sinful to use anything but black and white because color is of the world. Others wanted to obey the law.

The problem is that we have the world within us as well as outside us, meaning that we have an inner affinity for the world as well as an inner resistance to it. So really we can't leave the world, because it is part of us. But Jesus tells us that we are not called upon to do so. Rather, we are called to enter into the world and yet not be of it. This is a more difficult challenge than attempting to withdraw from it. We buy into the values of our culture probably more than we realize. We often reflect rather than remain in tension with its values, standards, and expectations. If we have grown up in our culture or at least live in it now, we can expect to be to some degree acculturated. We are wise to assume that is so until proved otherwise.

We also need to accept our acculturation. It is part of the self that God accepts and therefore that we can accept. We are much more likely to control our preferences for our culture's values if we accept that inclination than if we reject or deny it and then feel guilt and shame over it. Have you not caught yourself being secretly delighted by some achievement, when you supposedly do not rate that achievement very high by Christian standards? Of course. This is your ambivalence. For example, have you been particularly delighted when your child develops precociously in certain areas?

Today the hold our culture has on our thinking and evaluating is described as an addiction. Ann Wilson Schaef,[3] for example, describes our entire society as an addict because its values and priorities "hook" us. Usually we speak of addiction to substances like alcohol and drugs, but we can also be addicted to processes like making money, or seeking status or power, or possessions valued by our culture. As with alcoholism, so also with our addiction to our societal values, we can hope only for one-day-at-a-time freedom from our addiction. We look to our Higher Power, as a recovering alcoholic does, to give us the power to direct ourselves. By ourselves we are as powerless over the acculturation process as a drug addict is over cocaine.

Cultural Expectations and Values

What are some of the cultural expectations, values, and priorities that we hold in regard to parenting? One is that our culture favors an extrovert over an introvert child, a highly competitive over a noncompetitive child, a child who knows how to be popular as opposed to a child who is his or her own person.

Our Christian heritage inclines us to be reflective, to develop a relationship with ourselves, and to care about others, regardless of who they are. Our culture values a child who has his or her hand to the wind to know which way the wind is blowing. Our Christian heritage values integrity and loyalty though they may put us at cross purposes with current trends. These differing values may create conflicts, for adults as well as for children.

Another value our culture teaches is instant gratification, yet as parents we can see that waiting for a while or taking time to accomplish something may be more beneficial. Our children, however, often seem to want things as soon as their friends have them or they hear about them.

In general, our culture (particularly the media) has little interest in the spiritual side of life. Yet most people have spiritual longings but are not encouraged by our culture to explore them. Our children may sometimes feel different because they have a strong Christian faith in a basically secular culture.

We talk much about youth being overly influenced by their peers. What about us parents? Do we not feel peer pressure? When was the last time you spoke up about what you really believed when it would have endangered your relationship with the group? What about your courage regarding so-called controversial issues? Have you remained silent because speaking would have aroused negative feelings in the hearers? If so, you know how it is to feel and follow peer pressure.

Next we might ask how our culture evaluates success. Certainly one criterion for success is accumulation of money and possessions. When I (Bill) attended a high-school reunion recently, I was told by several in revered tones about one of our classmates who had become a millionaire. Another told me about his children.

He stressed the high salary of his youngest. "And he is only twenty-eight!" he said.

Another criterion for success is popular acclaim and prestige. But this, like accumulation of goods, depends on comparison with others. The spirit behind the standards, therefore, is competition. This may not leave much room for the Christian value of coop-eration.

How does Jesus' life rate according to these standards? According to our culture's standards, not very well. He could have had so much and he ended up with so little.

When Jesus' miracles were making him famous, his brothers wanted him to go to Jerusalem for the feast and do his miracles there, where the important people could see them. They told him, "For no one who wants to be widely known acts in secret." Fame was not one of his goals. "My time has not yet come, but your time is always here" (John 7:1-6).

When Jesus talked about values and priorities, he said the first will be last and the last will be first (Matt. 19:30). If this is so, for what are we competing? But the pressures were not easy for Jesus either. He took forty days and nights to prepare himself for the tensions and temptations that were before him in his calling as Messiah (Matt. 4:1-11). Perhaps it would be good for us parents also to take some time to go, like Jesus, to a "lonely place" and get ourselves straight on our values.

How the Media Help Shape Our Culture

The cultural conditioning that we and our children receive from the media is difficult to assess. No answers exist as to why some people are very susceptible to the media and others less. Today sophisti-cated polls produce accurate predictions about the media's effect. Advertisers know that the image must fit the receiver. We seem to live in a valueless society in which anything is all right as long as the producer of the product or the entertainment makes money.

This, of course, is not a new phenomenon, but it is new to have highly developed methods of manipulation brought into our homes at every hour of the day or night. We seldom know if our preferences have originated within us or have come from the bombardment of the media.

An example of the complexity of this issue is our culture's emphasis on violence, a value counter to the Christian faith. Movies, television, music, books, and comic books imply that violence is entertaining and that life is not exciting without it. Children are often attracted to violent toys, such as guns, weapon-toting action figures, and video games that are often based on the violent destruction of opponents—a child "kills" or "destroys" and thereby wins.

▼

We must decide what young people need to become fully functioning, capable adults.

Some sources speculate that forbidding such violence-based toys, games, movies, and other entertainment based on violence may increase their attraction. Parents and others who teach or work with children have two huge tasks ahead: trying to influence the media to reduce violence and trying to help children and youth learn more humane ways to solve problems.

Most of us have tried limiting the choice of the TV programs that enter our homes. Do our children even know that having a TV set, buying books, reading newspapers, and seeing the advertisements programmed for us is a choice? So accustomed are we to the place of media in the home that we probably do not even think of it as a choice.

We determined not to let the TV schedule our lives. We believe we give a strong message by where we place the TV. Is it where we eat? Where we sleep? In our living room? The TV will dominate any room it is in!

Is it any wonder that throughout the world, a TV set is the most popular piece of furniture? Only a few parents can justify the lack of a TV set without creating feelings of deprivation. Yes, parents too can be addicted to TV! Do you ever place a TV program above social contact? We have.

In a thought-provoking article, Robert D. Strom[4] states that one way to improve communication is in noting the most common activity in which children spend extended periods of time with parents. In 1985 three out of four parents watched TV with their children (Gallup). Strom observes that "during televiewing adults and children look at the same pictures and they hear the same words. But previous experience causes them to sometimes reach dissimilar conclusions. It is these differences in perception that enable family members to benefit from one another."

Strom's observations are a valuable way to stay in touch with TV's cultural conditioning of us and our children. If the program cannot be discussed immediately after its viewing, mealtime might be a good time.

Educators H. Stephen Glenn and Joel W. Warner[5] present an idea that makes much sense, namely that young people cannot be "rehabilitated" until they have become "habilitated." By "habilitation" they mean "developing the potential of people so that they can function capably and independently in the world." Many skills needed for obtaining and maintaining a job and for developing the moral maturity needed for parenting seem to be lacking today. "The recent incursion of technology and urbanization into our culture," say Glenn and Warner, "altered the family's ability to produce these experiences [of habituation]. We must decide what young people need to become fully functioning, capable adults." Most of the skills that they then identify concern communication within the family.

Using Mealtime Conversation

Today, because of unprecedented social and economic pressures on parents, teaching communication skills at home has to be intentional. In earlier times a family ate together because preparing food was such a laborious task. Today every person can prepare his or her food separately with the help of the supermarket, refrigerator, and microwave oven. In fact, many families find it necessary to have separate meals much of the time.

In one generation we have abolished a great amount of dependence upon gender roles. Our social critics have exposed the ills of gender-related behavior, but the disruption of these expectations in the home will take more than exposure to correct. Activities such as preparing food, doing laundry, and keeping the home clean produced a side benefit of working together on obviously necessary tasks. Now, however, we need to plan carefully the gathering of the family to communicate with each other. Today mealtime can sometimes provide that opportunity.

As a family we can use that time to discuss a TV program. We could begin by asking, "What did you see happening in that program?" Even children who cannot yet read can participate in this kind of discussion. Learning to observe accurately and to relate sequentially are important intellectual skills, and they are learned best in a group. It would be an unusual family if everyone saw the same things in a program. It is said that much of consumer advocate Ralph Nader's ability to think and analyze came from the mealtime discussions in his home. His father insisted that the children discuss issues of the day at the evening meal and that they challenge each other's opinions. If family members can listen to each other in this way, they will be learning self-disclosure. Even the way we view conflict is formed in our early experiences. If a child learns at home that conflict is too traumatic to engage in, the stress of not being true to oneself and not standing up for oneself when in disagreement can follow him or her into adulthood. On the other hand, when discussions are held and each person's opinion is respected even though one may differ, the child can learn to be true to his or her own viewpoint. Having to defend our position can teach responsibility and diffuse the suspicion that others are picking on us just to be mean. Parents need to take care to point out the differences that naturally exist in abilities to perceive and communicate at the different ages. Insensitive parents may unwittingly tolerate tyranny among siblings.

Obviously mealtime discussions can involve books and other media. We believe that a parent should read as many of their children's textbooks as possible. Even better, if both parents read the textbooks, the contents can be discussed so that all can participate. Then, if as often happens, the parents disagree about the appropriateness of the material, the children can see how adults can disagree and stay on the subject without resorting to name calling but can support their opinions with logical reasoning.

My (Lucy's) parents were farmers who always ate their meals with the family. As the youngest of six children, I can say that much of what I learned growing up was by listening to other siblings and parents discuss their experiences of the day at supper. I know I learned to hold my own in discussions from them. My mother did not let the cultural conditioning of her day push her to agree with my dad. Nor did my dad hesitate to argue persuasively his points. Their discussions were based on practical issues in their lives, and they were instructive to the children at the same time. In their verbal sparring there was much logical structure. I could spot a logical fallacy very early, although only through my later education did I find out the name for the process.

A young mother described to me (Lucy) her feelings when she read a book her daughter brought home that was geared for fourth-grade girls. It was from the school's shelf of recommended reading. To the mother's chagrin, the book's assumption was that boy-girl relationships were very important to a child of this age. They were not important to her child, and no one regarded the child as being behind in her development. Discussions with her daughter brought out the child's disinterest in relation to the book's content. The mother wanted her daughter to progress naturally to the stage of noticing boys rather than being pushed by cultural pressures.

Devotional reading material is well suited for family discussion, particularly at mealtime. Bible stories can be introduced from Scripture or from a good Bible story book. Most church libraries have these books and children can help with the selection. A regular practice of opening the material for discussion after its reading brings the relevance of Scripture to daily life. Parents and children who learn from each other develop a clearer understanding of their faith as well as of personal opinions and feelings.

Reading Aloud

Reading aloud is another skill that families can enjoy. We discovered that our youngest son was deficient in this skill when we asked him to read some devotional material at mealtime. Reading aloud develops articulation skills, and being read to develops listening skills. Sometimes people even as adults still do not listen and follow a conversation well.

I (Lucy) can still hear my third-grade teacher, Miss Elinor, reading each Friday another chapter of *Hans Brinker and the Silver Skates.* How exotic Hans seemed in his ability to glide on the frozen canal. Only by listening carefully could we picture the landscape and Hans in it. The whole room was completely quiet as we formed the pictures in our minds. How we hated to see the book close, even if we had been wishing to go home fifteen minutes earlier. I thank my teacher who led me to a lifetime appreciation of the use and sound of words. Perhaps our children will look back with similar fond memories of the times we read aloud together.

Making Choices

Discussing reading material or television programs is a time to examine hypothetical questions such as, "If these are the facts and these are my values, what are my choices?" Today we are pro-grammed by our culture to "have it all." This means to many of us that we do not have to choose anything that will mean giving up something else. Yet in reality, if we have "a" we often simply cannot have "b." Sentimentality often prevails when we become adults, and we try to give a disappointed child both "a" and "b."

Learning to be able to say, "I made the wrong choice, but I'll live," leads us toward maturity. The experiences of people who have gone before us teach us that both the seemingly good and the seemingly bad come from choices, but that God is involved in all of them. The story of Joseph in the Old Testament teaches us a universal lesson. When Joseph was sold into slavery by his jealous brothers, he suffered. Later when he was reconciled with his brothers he said, "Even though you intended to harm me, God intended it for good" (Gen. 15:20). Choice is a stern but reality-based teacher. We can become sounding boards for our children to talk over the many choices that become available to them.

▼

Things to Talk About and Do

1.   What childhood dream from your past may be directing your child now? What is its effect?

2.   In which area(s) are you embarrassed by your children's lack of accomplishment? Why?

3.   "In the world" is difficult to explain. Write two ways that a family might be "in the world." Repeat this, using "of the world."

4.   What have been your primary struggles with discipline? What has proven effective and constructive? What hasn't worked well?

5.   Where does your family buy into the cultural conditioning of TV? Are you satisfied with this conditioning?

6.   Write one story that you could tell your children from your years when you were their age. Let them read or share something of their experience that compares or contrasts with it.

▼

Notes

1.   Henri Nouwen, *Reaching Out* (Garden City, N.Y.: Doubleday, 1975).

2.   Ann Miller, *Prisoners of Childhood* (New York: Basic Books, 1981).

3.   Ann Wilson Schaef, *When Society Is an Addict* (New York: Harper, 1988).

4.   Robert D. Strom, "Expectations for Learning in the Future," *Journal of Creative Behavior* 23, no. 2 (1989): 126.

5.   H. Stephen Glenn and Joel W. Warner, *Developing Capable Young People* (Hurst, Texas: Humansphere, 1982).

▼▼

Adopting God's Model for Parenting

▲▲

Although historically we have referred to God as father, the qualities of mother have also been included in our understanding of God. Knowing we have a Heavenly Parent who also loves our children can be our support when faced with our own parental limitations.

God as our Heavenly Parent is the model for our parenting. As God loves and accepts us apart from our behavior, so also can we who have received this love give it to our children. As God calls us to responsibility, we can encourage our children to be responsible persons who accept the consequences of their actions.

God as Father and Mother

When I (Bill) was a student in seminary I taught a boys' Sunday school class in an inner-city mission. My supervisor told me that because most of these boys came from unstable families where the father was either absent or alcoholic, I would be wise not to put much emphasis on God as a father. Many years later as I teach seminary students I am told the same thing, but for a different reason: emphasizing God as father is too narrow a picture. In our need for human analogies we need to use both masculine and feminine images as Scripture does.

The gender applied to God, particularly in God's parental role, has been important throughout the church's history. The Roman Catholic church strongly emphasizes God as father, and their priests, all male, are addressed as father. Yet that church seeks a balance by exalting the Virgin Mary as one to whom to pray and has established influential orders of women headed by Mothers Superior. Protestant churches are less balanced in their emphasis on God as father but almost always refer to the church in feminine terms, and now most denominations ordain women clergy. Obviously we seem to need both genders for our conception of the deity, especially for nurturing images of God. For the real issue of God as a parent is that God is a nurturer.

Since we call God our creator, the image of father seems natural to many. When we address prayers to this Father, the image of God as nurturer becomes clearer, particularly the "Our Father" of the Lord's Prayer. This is the God who makes his face to shine upon us and gives us peace (Num. 6:25-26)—reassurance that enables trust. Although a female, I (Lucy) have had a positive image of God as father. It meant physical strength that could be depended on. It meant the providing of food and shelter, all qualities of my father. I was aware as a child that I was unable to provide any of these basics. But I did not think of God as one with whom to build a relationship. That concept occurred later and is still growing.

In scriptural descriptions of God's parental function, all the qualities of positive fatherhood and motherhood, masculinity and femininity, are included. In Psalm 103:13-14 God is described as a compassionate father: "As a father has compassion for his children, so the Lord has compassion for those who fear him. For he knows how we were made; he remembers that we are dust." This father knows and understands our limitations and frailties. In the New Testament this father is referred to as *Abba,* an Aramaic word for father that indicates affection. Jesus used it in addressing God, as did Paul, as an affectionate term that denoted childlike intimacy and trust. "God has sent the Spirit of his Son into our hearts crying 'Abba! Father!'" (Gal. 4:6). These references to God as a father emphasize the nurturing parent. When the prophet Isaiah, speaking for God, described God's faithfulness, he used the image of a mother: "Can a woman forget her nursing child, or show no compassion for the child of her womb? Even these may forget, yet I will not forget you" (Isa. 49:15).

When Jesus lamented over the resistant people of Jerusalem, he used a maternal image. "How often have I desired to gather your children together as a hen gathers her brood under her wings, and you were not willing!" (Matt. 23:37). No matter what the gender, the image is still the nurturing parent.

God is our nurturer in every stage of our life. Unlike the father and mother that we *leave* to become mature, this is the parent that we stay with to become mature. God's parenting is not simply preparatory but permanent. Paradoxically as we grow in our dependence on our Heavenly Parent, we become more mature.

▼

Having God as parent is a reminder that we are parents *under* God and are not God.

stay with to become mature. God's parenting is not simply preparatory but permanent. Paradoxically as we grow in our dependence on our Heavenly Parent, we become more mature.

This kind of dependency on and trust in God seems to come naturally to a child but not to adults. Adults are aware of the kind of world we live in, but children are not—unless subjected to severe abuse and alienation. This awareness leads to the break with innocence that shakes the adolescent's faith. There are good reasons for doubting both the goodness and the existence of God. To grow in trust within this milieu of doubt is the challenge of adult faith.

Accepting God's Perfect Parenthood

We need to take this trust of God as our parent into our parenting. This means that we envisage our parenthood within God's parenthood. Because the Heavenly Parent is our children's parent as well as ours, there is a potential for spiritual bonding as we look at the family within this perspective. To develop this trust so that it encompasses all of our parental concerns, we need to develop a relationship with our Heavenly Parent that can handle all of our emotions.

The story of Job's striving with God has meant much to me (Lucy) in this respect, although its meaning did not become clear at first. At first I found it an interesting story but not a metaphor for life. Job's relationship with God was so strong that Satan could challenge

God to test him. The apparent removal of God's favor from Job disrupted Job's relationship with God. He demanded to meet with God, saying that his trust had been destroyed. He expressed his angry feelings openly to God.

Job's trust in God is like mine. I accepted God's benevolence, but when it seemed withdrawn, I have said, like Job, "Come and quarrel with me." For it seemed that I had been the target of God's special testing.

The outcome of the testing was acceptance of God's perfect parenthood. So much is God involved with us that the image given for his care is that he knows the number of our hairs (Matt. 10:30). So much is God involved in our environment that even the dispensable sparrow is inventoried (Matt. 10:29). When we are related to God as a parent we are not like some scientists who think God is the creator of the universe but who see no place for this creator's continued involvement with creation. God as parent is one who has us and ours firmly within God's nourishing care.

Accepting Our Limitations
and Our Limited Dreams

Having God as parent is a reminder that we are parents *under* God and are not God. We may not think we need any reminders of our limitations as parents. The frustrations are enough to make us feel inadequate more often than we would like. But feeling inadequate and recognizing our limitations are not the same. Feeling inadequate is a negative reminder of defeat. Awareness of our limitations is a starting point for trust.

It is especially helpful to keep our limitations in mind in our images of who and what our children should be. It is good to have such pictures—and perhaps they will help us shape our goals as parents—but they can be detrimental both to our children and to our relationships with them if they become the standard by which we measure our children and accept them. We are less likely to do this when we are aware that our children also have a Heavenly Parent whose pictures of our children may be different from ours. As God said through the prophet Isaiah, "For my thoughts are not your thoughts, nor are your ways my ways, says the Lord. For as the heavens are higher than the earth, so are my ways higher than your ways, and my thoughts than your thoughts" (Isa. 55:8-9).

Our dreams for our children are strongly influenced by the images of children currently accepted by our culture. When these cultural pictures are our guide, we expect our child to fit the mold, and this hinders us from becoming acquainted with who our child really is and with his or her gifts. We then have difficulty enjoying the child and constantly check to see if he or she is conforming to what we want to see.

▼

Our dreams for our children are strongly influenced by the images of children currently accepted by our culture.

Wishing our children to conform to culturally conditioned images has always affected parents, but the advent of ever more sophisticated media has complicated the issue. Educator William F. Fore points out: "The whole process of television is providing us with a worldview which not only determines what we think but also how we think and who we are."[1] It shapes our dreams and our dreams tell us what is acceptable and what is not. We seldom can act upon an independent dream. For example, think for a moment about the dreams you have had for yourself. How many of these dreams have originated with you? How many have come from your home of origin? How many have come from our cultural ideals? And even those from your home of origin were probably culturally engendered.

Some of our dreams for ourselves may have been helpful. Others we may even smile about because they are so far removed from present reality. So it is wise to know when to let a dream go. The same goes with our images for our children. When they do not fit—and particularly when they only contrast with the real world—we need to let them go. In fact, letting go of these pictures or dreams for our children is fundamental to letting our *children* go. Because they ultimately will need to leave us, it is important that we let them leave.

John Stanley[2] poignantly speaks about the pain of a parent's dream and the need to let it go:

> My dream involves my daughter. I so clearly envisioned the path she should travel. My wife and I knew the pitfalls on the road of life, the rougher spots where a detour would smooth out the route, and also the stretches of delightfully smooth travel. But sometimes my daughter wouldn't listen.
>
> Many times she wouldn't listen.
>
> "Drink the milk, sweetheart, it's good for you," as she gleefully poured it on the floor. "I *told* you not to pull on that," as I applied the bandage. "Of *course* you can't have a cookie before dinner.
>
> "Have you finished all your homework?" as she plopped down in front of the TV, nodding assent. Later we received the "incompletes" from the teachers. "What do you mean, you want to quit the swimming team? Sure it's hard work, but that won't hurt you." She quit.

John Stanley goes on to describe her adolescence with boyfriends, school, and other problems, none of them according to the dream. The wishes for her to be active in church and college and to meet a fine young man and have a big church wedding go unmet. He finally admits he hates the dream and calls it a detriment to his life. He bids it goodbye, telling it to bury itself in the furthest reaches of his mind where he can never recall it again:

> And when you are gone, old Dream, I will repair the bridge to my loved one, and I will dash across it and sweep up my daughter in my arms. Then I will say "I still love you and always will, sweetheart. *Nothing* can change that. I would have told you sooner, but a Dream got in the way."

Adopting God as Our Parental Model

Having God as our parent is also our model for parenting. God gives unconditional love (agape). This love is the essence of the gospel, namely that "in Christ God was reconciling the world to himself" (2 Cor. 5:19). God the Father reaches out to his children through his Son Jesus. God became one of us as Jesus lived among us. Through Jesus' life, death, and resurrection, God extends to all of us complete and total reconciliation so that we can feel completely at ease in God's presence. Nothing in all creation can separate us from God. Through God's covenant with us in our baptism, God assures us of God's unconditional love by a forgiveness that is always present. We are fully secure in our relationship with our Heavenly Parent.

We who have received and experienced this unconditional love from God have the privilege of passing it on to our children. As God accepts us just the way we are and not as we should be, so we can accept our children as they are and not as we have hoped they would be. As our Heavenly Parent accepts our *person* while disapproving or approving of our *behavior,* so we can accept the person of our child even though we do not care at all for his or her behavior at the moment. As God's approval or disapproval of our behavior has nothing to do with God's acceptance of us as persons, so our disapproval or approval of our child's behavior need have nothing to do with our love and acceptance of the child.

In the world, however, acceptance is tied to behavior—how we perform and what we accomplish. So even if our love for our children remains unconditional when we disapprove of their behavior, we need to tell them we love them. Children need to hear this because they may perceive rejection when we express disapproval of their behavior. So they need to hear again and again that we love them to believe it. We also need to hear again and again that our Heavenly Parent loves us to believe it. This is why we listen to the preached Word at church and receive the Sacrament of Holy Communion. These are God's ways of reassuring us that God's love is unconditional—and that we are accepted by grace and not by our good behavior or successful accomplishments. The words "I love you" help our children to feel secure in our presence. We need to say them again and again. When we think of God as our model parent, we are more likely to model God's love in our families. We need to remind ourselves again and again of our model, particularly when a child's behavior is "getting to us."

God's unconditional love is coupled with a call to responsibility. As parents we want our children to understand the same love and call to responsibility. The belief that we have caused and chosen all of the things that have happened to us is cause for despair and we can reject it. With the umbrella of God's forgiveness over us, we can accept this responsibility, knowing also that we are limited human beings.

▼

When we think of God as our model parent, we are more likely to model God's love in our families.

Sometimes the idea of unconditional love is equated with indulgence, implying that we can have accomplishments without work, get to destinations without a journey, and have skills without practice. Indulgence leads only to lack of confidence, because children feel inadequate before tasks that require effort. All of us make our own choices and bear the consequences. So our children need to know from the beginning that the forgiveness and love we have from God does not exclude consequences. When a precious item is broken, for example, it no longer has the form it once had. Replacing the item does not mean that the original was not broken. Without this realization, we would not learn to mourn losses.

An eight-year-old boy, fascinated by airplanes, begged his parents to buy him a radio-controlled model. Instead of buying him one of the expensive and fragile toys or simply saying no, the parents put the responsibility on his shoulders. They told him that he could save his own allowance and buy a plane if he wished to, but they also warned him how easily such a toy could crash and be gone forever.

Undaunted, the boy saved much of his allowance over a period of months. He then picked out a model that he could afford. His parents selected a safe place for him to test-fly it. The plane took off without any difficulty, and the boy had a great time flying it around the field and doing acrobatic maneuvers. Unfortunately, he lacked skill in landing, and the fragile plastic plane pancaked into the runway.

It was an expensive lesson, but how much better to learn it from a radio-controlled model airplane than from something more dangerous! By granting their son a measure of freedom along with responsibility, they helped him learn about effort, consequences, good judgment, and mourning one's losses.

In earlier eras, the link between actions and consequences might have been more easily taught. Going out in cold weather to bring in wood for a fire kept the house warm. In many families this chore belonged to the children. It was easy to see the consequences if they handled this responsibility well or poorly. No wood, no fire, no heat!

Today parents must look for situations that will teach their children responsibility. Doing so may be the most creative task that parents have. There are many possibilities, and they will vary according to age. Preschoolers can help pick up toys at the end of the day and put them away, or help clean up their own messes. School-age children can set and clear the table, help with dishes, clean their rooms, do laundry, help cook meals, sort and take out recycling items, or mow the lawn. Assigning regular, specific tasks works well in many families, with some rotation of tasks to provide relief and variety.

It is certainly easier for the parents to do most of these tasks, but the children then lose opportunities to learn responsibility. An older child may wish to entertain company. He or she can do so by prepar-ing the house for the guests.

In our generation the children have often had more privileges and material goods than their parents did. We have often heard, "I did without; my children will not." That often causes parents to have fulfillment in providing things that the children have not asked for. Lessons in skills in which the parents never felt they had succeeded were pushed on the child. Even the child's responsibil-ity to ask was taken away. In more subtle ways this need to give to our children more than we had is still going on. If we watch and pray to see what our children are really interested in, we can match our support with their responsibility and preferences.

We are called by God to care for ourselves, for others, and for our environment. As we help our children to do these things, we are also helping them to develop their own self-esteem through having confidence in their abilities. The blessing of God's forgiveness is coupled with the blessing of God's calling.

By teaching and supporting responsibility we are preparing our children to leave us. The family setting is the preparation for life on one's own. The process begins as early as a child can share in the responsibility of family living.

▼

Things to Talk About and Do

1. Do you remember being told by your parents that they loved you? If they didn't say so often, how did you know they loved you? Were there other signs of affection? Did they do things for you or provide things for you?

2. Recall the story of the boy and the plane. What experiences have your children had that helped them discover the consequences of their actions? Recall some from your own childhood.

3. God reassures us that we are loved and forgiven. How does this knowledge help you in your parenting? Name some specific situations in which you need to remind yourself that God is loving you, guiding you, and forgiving you.

▼

Notes

1. William F. Fore, *Television and Religion* (Minneapolis: Augsburg, 1987), 22.

2. John Stanley, "I Cannot Tell My Daughter that I Love Her," *Minneapolis Tribune*, 4 Aug., 1979, 5B.

▼▼▼

3

Giving Consistent Signals

▲▲

Parents who give double signals to their children in their rules and regulations are undermining their own parental authority. Behind the double signal is the double mind (James 1:8). When we are of two minds about our directives, our communication is often confused.

To give clear signals we need to end our vacillation and resolve our double-mindedness. Our commitment to God helps us in this task. We can come to God in prayer when we are double-minded, asking for help and guidance. Our thinking then becomes more integrated in a flexible way, and our decision will reflect our thoughtful attention. The power of single-mindedness that comes from commitment to God is communicated through our actions and words.

What Is Behind the Double Signal?

Susan was leaving for her circle meeting and gave Bob a few last-minute instructions for three-year-old Jessica. "Remember, Bob, her bedtime is eight o'clock. Please see that she gets in bed by then."

"Oh, sure, Susan" said Bob. "We'll do that, won't we Jessica?"

"No," said Jessica.

Bob and Susan both had to smother a laugh, but Susan also felt an ominous pain. Jessica was probably right!

Bob was extremely fond of his little daughter and enjoyed reading to her. At eight o'clock he closed the book. "Remember, Mom said you are to be in bed by eight o'clock."

"No," said Jessica once more. "Read another one."

Bob gave himself away when he blamed Susan for reminding them of the rules. He was simply carrying out her orders. Sharp little Jessica had learned already that Bob liked to indulge her. She had talked him out of his directives many times. Bob finally tucked Jessica in by 8:45. Jessica had once again correctly read his double signal: "Go to bed, bedtime is eight o'clock, but you can stretch that out for at least a half hour."

Is this not a minor matter? What really is the difference between Jessica's being in bed by eight o'clock and enjoying another forty-five minutes with her dad? Being in bed by eight o'clock, however, is not the real issue here. The real issue is that Jessica is learning that her father gives double signals in his directives. And while Jessica exploits this tendency of Bob's, she is also confused by it. The logic of St. Paul is to the point. "If [the flute or harp] do not give distinct notes, how will anyone know what is played?" "If the bugle gives an indistinct sound, who will get ready for battle?" (1 Cor. 14:7-8).

An even bigger issue for Bob is that behind his confusing double signals is a double mind. St. James calls a person like Bob double-minded and unable to keep a steady course (James 1:8 NEB). In one mind, Bob thinks it is a good idea for Jessica to be in bed by eight o'clock as long as Susan enforces it. But his other mind says he would feel better if he did not have to enforce something that his daughter does not want. He would rather not be the one to cause her unhappiness. If he puts her to bed by eight o'clock against her will and she cries, he feels guilty. Could Bob be secretly indulging the "little boy" within?

St. James says that a double mind indicates instability stemming from a lack of identity (James 1:7). We can see this in Bob's confusing picture of his identity as Jessica's father.

Another word for double-mindedness is ambivalence, a word from Latin that means two opposing strengths. Because the two minds or strengths oppose each other, they hinder any integrated action. Obviously "mind" in this instance means more than intellect because double-mindedness is rooted deeply in our person.

James alludes to this when he says, "Purify your hearts, you double-minded" (4:8). The heart too is involved, the symbolic seat of our feelings and passions.

Being True to Ourselves

Bob said he would do as Susan requested and put Jessica to bed by eight. But Bob shut his mind to the subliminal awareness that he also wanted Jessica to stay up longer if she wished. Bob preferred to be an old softie with his daughter rather than a rule enforcer. Susan could have that job! But his wish worked behind his back where it was more effective in sabotaging the eight o'clock bedtime than if he used his conscious judgment. Have you ever said yes to something to which you also wanted to say no? What effect did your no have on your having said yes?

One indication that we are acting contrary to our intent is fatigue. It is so easy to get bored and tired when we are doing something we don't want to do. A second indication is crotchetiness. We are angry at ourselves for saying yes and therefore easily scapegoat others in the process as an outlet for our annoyance. A third indication is procrastination. Have you noticed how hard it is to be on time for an event to which you really didn't want to go? Then in addition we expect gratitude for saying and doing yes!

As we have seen, this double mind shows itself when we give double signals to our children. We can say no in ways that seem to give them permission, as Bob did. Or we can say yes in ways that say, "Better not!" In contrast to this confusing double-mindedness, Jesus said, "Let your word be 'Yes, Yes,' or 'No, No'; anything more than this comes from the evil one" (Matt. 5:37).

Expecting Resistance

Because of this tension between our two minds, we may act as though we don't expect our child to obey, as though we don't expect our child to take our rules or our requests seriously—at least not right away. Because we anticipate a struggle, one is more likely to occur.

Some of us develop the habit of associating resistance with rules and directives. This inclination comes from our own childhood memories. Like Bob we feel guilty if our child obeys us immediately. We fear that we are inhibiting the child's individuality. Is all this actually a resistance to accepting parental authority? Children, like others, tend to live up to expectations. So they help us to maintain the "security of the familiar." If we feel more comfortable with resistance, they may well provide it. So the confusion perpetuates itself.

The problem with double-mindedness about supposedly minor rules like bedtime is that this kind of confusion extends to the more important issues and specifically into the tension over being in the world but not of it (see chapter 1). If going to bed on time is unpleasant, so also is being true to our values as children of God when others pressure us to compromise. Can we parents tolerate *this* unpleasantness for our children? If the confusion in parental signals also extends, at least in the child's mind, to this tension of being in but not of the world, can it lead to the child's confusion over his or her spiritual identity?

▼

If we are to cease giving double signals, we need to do something about the double-mindedness behind them.

The Importance of Clear Messages

As a young parent, I (Lucy) had not had the experience of being comfortable with authority. I had been a high school teacher who found discipline very hard to maintain. My security was further battered because I taught in a difficult school where there was no base of respect for discipline. In addition, my personal views of authority were confused. I needed more personal growth before I could make the crucial distinction between discipline and punishment.

For family settings, discipline can be defined as a method applied by adults to help children learn to control behavior so that they can grow up to accomplish what their set of values tells them is right. The internalization of discipline leads to a satisfying life in which persons learn to think for themselves and to care for others at the same time. Clear messages, not double signals, are necessary before one can internalize discipline.

The lifelong journey of the Christian is part of this internalization process. The model we wish to impart to our children and others is this: that our actions are congruent with our beliefs.

I (Lucy) was often confused between wanting the children to be free to choose their course of action and wanting to decide for them. I did not like to face the fact that in some cases there was no real choice for the children. The decision really rested upon my parental authority. Now I realize that it can take a lifetime to sort out authentic choices from illusionary choices.

It is easy to think that nothing has gone right when we parent. Some of this comes from our cultural conditioning that says that parents are responsible for everything. Some of it also comes from the terminology we use. A good example is the way we currently use the word "dysfunctional" in reference to families. Many people have told us sadly that they "come from dysfunctional families." Therapist Jean Illsley Clarke[1] suggests that we change this term to "uneven," which removes the element of blame and leaves us with a descriptive term. This term could make us more comfortable in examining and recognizing our parental style without becoming defensive. Because it is rare today that both parents come from the same background, they almost always find it necessary to work through and examine their family parenting styles. "Uneven" allows us to be on a mutual footing. Bob and Susan can come out even instead of being in a power struggle over Bob's double-mindedness.

The unconscious part of the mind influences us more strongly than the conscious mind. Hardly anything in our lives is unaffected by the unconscious mind. Marriage counselor Harville Hendrix[2] has some remarkable insights for us. Although his book is about the role of the unconscious in the relationship between a man and a woman, much of what it says also applies to parenting. Our automatic reactions confuse us. They do not always match what we thought we were doing. Using neuroscientist Paul McLean's model, Hendrix refers to the brain stem, which is the most primitive area of the brain controlling most of our automatic reactions, as the "old brain." It is where many past memories with heavy emotional content are stored. The "new brain" is the site of our cognitive, conscious functioning. When we parent, we receive unexpected messages from the old brain that can frustrate our conscious planning.

Pastoral counselor William Miller explores this same phenomenon from a similar point of view. Using the model of psychoanalyst Carl G. Jung, Miller urges us to be aware of our shadow. Our shadow is the unconscious portion of ourselves that gives rise to dark urges, often negative and frightening, that we do not understand. They come from the dark side of our unconscious—the old brain. When our shadow interferes with our straight thinking and sends a dangerous double signal, it is time to become aware of the contents of our dark side. Says Miller, "Closing your eyes in the darkness neither increases your safety nor improves your vision."[3]

The limits of parental authority are usually not clear today. However, clear signals can be given only by someone who accepts parenthood as a position of authority. In some cultures the authority pattern is almost the opposite to ours. More than one of my (Lucy's) Nigerian students has told me that in most of Africa any adult can exercise authority with any child. They are amazed that there would be any other way. And we are equally amazed by their way. Parental authority is on shaky ground here because we do not respect authority for authority's sake.

Why are we surprised that parents would be confused about authority?

Discipline and authority go together. The ideal would be that our children receive clear messages from us so that eventually they can internalize them and have wisdom enough to reject any authority that directs them against their moral values.

Resolving Our Double-Mindedness

If we are to cease giving double signals, we need to do something about the double-mindedness behind them. The spiritual identity that we wish for our children can be our means for overcoming our double-mindedness. This takes us again to an identity larger than ourselves.

We are motivated to do things differently from our accustomed way if we believe that God is calling us to change. Then we are not in the project alone and can resolve our double-mindedness by sensing God's overtures. We are not *alone* because we are not our *own*. We belong to God. We are committed to God. As St. Paul said, "You are not your own; you were bought with a price. So glorify God in your body" (1 Cor. 6:19-20 RSV). We need to face up to both minds and give God an open mind, allowing God to lead us in ways compatible with both our identity and our calling.

It is our commitment to God that integrates our thinking and action. We are called as a parent and are committed to that call. We give clearer signals in parenting when we sense our parenting as our calling and see our role within the perspective of God, our Higher Parent. As Christians we have thrown in our lot with Christ. We are "God's own people" (1 Pet. 2:9). The King James version translates this as "a peculiar people." We are *different* in a constructive way. Here is then an identity that can both help us face our double-mindedness and resolve it.

When Double-Mindedness Can Be Good

There is power in single-mindedness or wholeheartedness. What we do with our whole heart is reinforced by our positive feelings. Perhaps this is why St. Paul describes his version of single-mindedness by the word "heartily." "Whatever your task, work heartily" (Col. 3:23 RSV).

But we may have a problem with power and be double-minded about it. No one wants to be powerless, but it has its advantages. There is no accountability if one is powerless. Responsibility goes with power, yet there is also satisfaction in exerting power. But that satisfaction can be distorted. So power is obviously a perilous resource for flawed people—and we are all flawed.

What protects us from misuse of power is again our commitment in which we accept power as a trust from God. As we say in the Lord's Prayer, "Thine is the kingdom, the power and the glory." So we are stewards of God's power. We "manage" it under God. As God's people we have been given power not only as parents, but in all aspects of our calling.

The power of single-mindedness comes from communicating in a consistent, clear way. Children, who are experts at picking up all aspects of communication, pick up our single-mindedness along with the words of the directive. The children hear a clear signal and are predisposed to give a positive response. We can actually expect that what we say will be taken seriously.

Single-mindedness should not be confused with stubbornness, although they have similarities. While single-mindedness, as we have described it, is commitment-oriented, stubbornness is ego-oriented.

As Bob was an example of double-mindedness, Joe's stubbornness took an inflexible negative cast. As a parent he was more likely to say "better not" when his children asked his permission. Joe found his power in blocking and restraining others, not only at home but in all his social roles.

▼

When Joe's two teenagers asked him if they could go on a week-long trip to a distant vacation spot sponsored by the church's youth group, they knew from past experience that he would say no and he did. But this time the older teen became emboldened and asked why.

Joe bristled and muttered something like, "Because I said so, that's why!"

"C'mon Dad," the teen persisted. "You've got to have some reason." "All right," Joe shot back. "It's for your safety. I'm not going to have you riding with any of those kids whose parents are foolish enough to give them their cars—or even with that young couple who is your sponsor."

It is our commitment to God that integrates our thinking and action. We are called as a parent and are committed to that call.

The teenagers told the sponsors about their father's objection. The young couple, however, had already been concerned about the safety factor and had decided to charter a bus with a professional driver.

Joe's teenagers were delighted. "Dad," they said, "it's not the way you think. The group has hired a bus with a professional driver."

"I've already said no," Joe replied sternly.

"But, Dad, you said—"

"Never mind what I said," Joe exploded. "I also said no."

Joe is single-minded all right, but irrationally so. Why can't he adjust to the new information? Because Joe does not negotiate. To him flexibility is a sign of weakness. His rigid single-mindedness or stubbornness is not based on reason but on an emotional defense system. For Joe to change his mind or to admit that he is wrong would threaten his fragile ego.

Joe's stubbornness is a sign of weakness, not strength. Inwardly he feels insecure, but the illusion of strength in stubbornness enables him to deny his insecurity. He fortifies his illusion of strength by saying no. Although he can't see it, his problem lies in his resistance to rethinking, reevaluating, considering new evidence, or negotiating.

For parents like Joe, a little double-mindedness in the sense of flexibility would be a good thing. For the issues of parenting are not as simple as his stubbornness would imply. For example, of what value will Joe's stubborn strength be when his children are too big and independent for him to control? Joe can make decisions easily because he resists looking into the complexity of the issues. He makes his decisions fast to avoid his subconscious fear of indecision. The decision is fixed because to reopen it would bring up all the fears that his immediate decision had forestalled.

Though we have been referring to double-mindedness in a negative way as vacillation, it can be a good response. It is negative only when it inhibits us from taking decisive action, and moves us to give double signals. But there are times when it is good not to take immediate action and instead to seek more information. In these instances, double-mindedness may be a needed step to making a good decision. Being double-minded in itself is not a sin.

Jesus was extremely double-minded in the garden of Gethsemane the night before his crucifixion. For three years he had been telling his disciples that his ministry would lead to his death, and it was they who objected. Now that his death was imminent, it was Jesus who was objecting. In his agony he prayed a most unusual prayer. "My Father, if it is possible, let this cup pass from me" (Matt. 26:39a). He was asking God to spare him from the cross. But he also had another prayer: "Yet not what I want, but what you want" (Matt. 26:39b).

What did Jesus do about his double-mindedness? He faced it consciously and openly, even though it was agonizing for him to do so. Then by sharing his double mind, his two desires, with God in prayer, putting each mind into a petition, he was able to make a decision. "My Father, if this cannot pass unless I drink it, your will be done" (Matt. 26:42). Having so prayed, Jesus arose and was prepared to face his death.

When as a parent you realize you are double-minded in a matter, take a good, hard look at what is involved. Is your double-mindedness due to the complexity of the issue or to some unfinished business from your past? Pray over the situation and try putting both minds, both possibilities, into petitions. This often clears the confusion so that you can decide which mind to affirm. It may help also to discuss your double-mindedness with your spouse or another trusted friend. When we know what we want, we will help our children as well as ourselves.

Decisions based on commitment rather than ego or past unmet needs free us to admit our mistakes, even to our children, because we ourselves are free to see them. None of us will always make the right decision. We are finite, flawed, and sometimes distortedly subjective. But we can always face our mistakes and change our minds accordingly.

▼

Decisions based on commitment rather than ego or past unmet needs free us to admit our mistakes, even to our children.

Accepting the Responsibility for Discipline

"Who's in charge here?" This is a question often asked in social confusion. Parents who are struggling with accepting their authority as parents may leave a vacuum in the area of who's in charge. Children are quick to fill it, to their parents' detriment. In this confusion the patterns of our parental homes can cast a long shadow over us. Most of us identify strongly either by emulation of or resistance to what we knew in the past. Because these impressions are stored in the "old brain," it is not until a situation in our parenting arises that our memories are triggered, causing different reactions in each parent. The parents then clash as each assumes a role from his or her family of origin.

The ideal situation is to achieve a democratically governed family in which each member experiences freedom commensurate with his or her authority so that each feels comfortable with him- or herself and desire to cooperate with others. Children can use their limited freedom more effectively when they are assured of their parents' authority. Achieving this goal of a democratic family takes much planning, and our awareness of the influence from our childhood homes is an important factor in this planning. If we avoid judgments regarding others' backgrounds and instead emphasize appreciation, we can be more objective in our planning and so accomplish more. As we parents communicate in a democratic way, we can decide what we would like to keep and what we would like to change from our childhood homes. This means that the basic rules for family living come from the consensus between the parents and the children, with room for negotiation in the minor rules.

Our homes of origin affect our children quite directly because our parents are the grandparents of our children. It is important for our maturity that we seek to establish a peer relationship with our parents. By so doing we will give them no more power over us than any other loved friend: we want to hear what they have to say regarding our parenting, but we need to take the responsibility for accepting or rejecting their suggestions. We believe that the grandparents in today's society—of which we are two—are able to accept this position. This emancipation from residual influences from our childhood homes frees us to act in wisdom rather than on impulse in the disciplining of our children.

As mentioned previously, feeling mature and capable as a parent is not easy. Childbirth itself often brings regression. Wise persons, grandparents included, are those who know just how to support the mother without implying that she is incapable at the moment. Today many social agencies are trying to meet this need for support of parents. The coffee klatch of young mothers served that function for me (Lucy). We met weekly and talked, among other things, about our parenting. (Amazingly, we are still meeting, although now we are a couples' group and talk a lot about our grandparenting.) Though this group assisted me greatly as a young parent, I believe today's organized support groups are better. They have better information and capable leadership. Nothing is more helpful than the support of those whose lives are under the same stresses and challenges as ours.

When children reach adolescence, they can be particularly confused—and tempted—by double-minded signals. If adolescent children today seem to be different from the children you had known before, it is because they are. That easily managed child may now decide to test the limits.

Some parents of easily managed children say that their children will not rebel as adolescents. We are not so sure about that. Joe's children were easily managed because he intimidated them. But already his teenage son is beginning to question openly his father's role. Adolescent rebellion is a natural component of growth. Those strong enough to rebel in adolescence know themselves better and may not develop so hostile a temperament, because they have acted on these natural feelings at the appropriate time of life.

Naturally this is not a pleasant time for those parents who are not happy having their authority questioned. Nor is it always a happy time even for those who do accept this questioning. If it is possible to turn that burst of adolescent energy into creative channels that build self-esteem, all will be better for it. Society used to be more helpful in this respect by having a structured place for young people's efforts. Parents need to use their creativity to provide healthy opportunities for the energy of adolescence. Because the readiest place for adolescent expression is sex, and because rebellion, if not handled wisely, can obliterate sexual control boundaries, we will need to deal with this in a separate chapter.

▼

Things to Talk About and Do

1.   In order to recognize double-minded messages in yourself or others, read through the following four messages which illustrate parental double signals. Some of the words given might be spoken, others implied. Which of these sound a little like you?

    a.   "Be yourself. Think for yourself. Be your own person. But don't lose out. Stay with the right people. Be with the kids that count. Don't identify with the losers. Be liked."

    b.   "Don't you dare!" But the facial expression may imply, "I don't expect you to behave. I expect challenge. I really like little rascals."

    c.   "Share with me where you are. Be honest. You can tell me anything. But don't say anything I don't want to hear, or I'll prove you wrong."

    d.   "I'm a self-sacrificing parent. I would do anything for you. But I expect you to be grateful!"

  Both parents should discuss these messages. Remember that the purpose is to understand double messages and decide how to revise them, rather than to make anyone feel devalued.

2.   Think of examples in your interaction with your children when you may have been double-minded like Bob or too stubborn like Joe. What has helped you find a good balance?

▼

Notes

1.   Jean Illsley Clarke, *Growing Up Again* (San Francisco: Harper & Row, 1989), 1.

2.   Harville Hendrix, *Getting the Love You Want* (New York: Henry Holt & Co., 1988).

3.   William Miller, *Make Friends with Your Shadow* (Minneapolis: Augsburg, 1981), 71.

▼▼

4

Dealing with Our Limitations: What Are Parental Powers?

▲▲▲

We have a difficult time in our culture determining what parental powers are. Sometimes we get the impression that parents are all-powerful in shaping their children, that they are like gods. Thus we have not only much blaming of parents today, but also much parental guilt. Neither is much help in parenting. When I asked a friend about a current film, he said, "It's a story of a troubled and misunderstood boy and his rigid and arbitrary father. It's another of those blame-the-parents films." Even if he were overstating the point, it shows his sensitivity as a parent to this prevalent cultural view.

Facing Our Limitations

Freudian psychology may have begun the trend in this blaming process, especially the blaming of the mothers. This trend came into full force in the 1950s and 1960s. Following World War II, technological advances in homemaking, advances in pediatric medicine, and planned parenthood seemed to make parenting easier. The utopian dream of rearing children easily seemed within grasp, and a large number of articulate and educated parents were ready to accept these advantages. At that time, motherhood was seen as a married woman's primary occupation. These changes set the stage for blaming parents, and particularly mothers, when things did not work out as anticipated. Mothers of a previous generation were perceived as having done the best they could under very trying circumstances. And if a child did something wrong, the question was not, "What's wrong with the parents?" but "How could he do such a thing to his parents?" The mothers from the 1950s to the present have been held accountable for just about everything, by themselves as well as society.

With so many advantages available to parents, the mother was seen as the causal factor in childrearing. Freud had spelled out for the psychology books the effects of the mother's influence of the child. How could the mother not be guilty if her efforts did not produce the expected perfection? Many mothers slid right into it! They were eager for the advances, and those who provided them had a ready-made audience.

Many other influences besides the parents affect a child's development. The shaping process and the child's own developing sense of responsibility are always shared with others, such as friends, teachers, and the media. While parents are not all-powerful gods, they are still potent influences in their parental care and encouragement.

A man who is now president of a college had a serious case of polio as a child. The doctors said that he would never walk again. His mother, however, defied that prognosis. Every day she forced her little son to move and exercise his legs. He admits that he hated her at the time for forcing him to do what was so hard and painful to do. Today, however, if you didn't know the story, you would not notice his slight limp. He feels a great deal differently now about his mother and her determination that he *would* walk.

A woman now active in an organization that helps people who cannot afford sufficient medical care says she was profoundly influenced by her father, a dentist. He left home for one month every summer to contribute his skills to a clinic in South America. She admits that as a child she resented his absence part of every summer, but as time went by, she realized the great importance of his gift and what a self-giving, concerned man her father was.

Both of these examples show the powerful influence parents can have, even though most of us have not been involved in such dramatic actions. But small kindnesses such as letting a car in ahead of us on a highway, or being careful not to disturb a bird and her nest even though they are in the way, can influence our children as well. I (Lucy) recall my farmer father mowing around a killdeer's nest rather than mowing through it and destroying it. In fact, many times parents are surprised when their children describe such incidents, long forgotten by the parents, that affected the children's values and the direction of their lives.

Parental authority used to be taken for granted. For many centuries in most cultures, children were expected to comply completely with parental wishes. For instance, Beatrix Potter, creator of Peter Rabbit, was expected to obey and cater to the demands of her Victorian parents long after she became an adult. They did not encourage her writing, despite her great talent. When she was in her forties, she finally left home and married, but even then her parents considered her marriage to be an inconvenience.

▼

One of the challenges of parenthood is to balance parental authority with encouragement for our children to make their own decisions.

One of the challenges of parenthood is to balance parental authority with encouragement for our children to make their own decisions. Young children have not yet had enough experience to make decisions that have long-term effects. Our children are developing individuals whose behavior and ideas are uneven. Only by carefully observing a child's development can we come near to satisfying ourselves that we are firm enough in authority to give the child security and flexible enough to hear clearly the child's preferences. Many parents whose children are involved in sports, the arts, or other skills requiring practice ask questions like this: "Do I make my child practice when he or she refuses? Then how do I encourage the spontaneity which is so necessary for what he or she is learning to do?"

Realizing that we have a Heavenly Parent reduces the stress of the responsibility that goes with our parental authority. We are not in the job alone. God also is parenting our children. And because God is God, our Heavenly Parent may not only see things differently from us human parents, but also may see more. In our moments of parental concern we can be comforted realizing that God may see more options than we see.

Just keeping our minds open to these realities often helps us see more options ourselves. It is so easy to get locked into either-ors and other limited viewpoints when we feel all alone in our vulnerability and fallibility.

Our relationship with our Heavenly Parent establishes our trust. Although sometimes we think our petitions are not answered very satisfactorily, we can continue to focus on our children in our prayers. On the one hand we bring our children to God who is their Heavenly Parent, and on the other hand we bring ourselves to God as human parents of our children. At these moments we can hear the words: "Be still, and know that I am God!" (Ps. 46:10). The limitations of our parenthood become very clear. Under these circumstances we are humbled. God is the giver and nurturer of life; we are but the ones who distribute the gift.

This response is in no way resignation. Rather it is action exemplifying our trust in God. In this attitude of trust in our Heavenly Parent and in our limited freedom, we have peace. It is a peace that comes from knowing that God has a larger view.

Another way of looking at our limited freedom is by the analogy of the left and right brains. With our left brain we function with the deposits of logic derived from our experience, and with our right brain we function beyond this logic with intuition. In our left brain we use reason and science, and in our right brain we use poetry, music, and the arts. We trust our Heavenly Parent to guide us in the use of both sides of our brain.

The Child's View of God

A small child's view of God is closely related to the child's view of his or her parents. A child's impression of its parents is usually the child's first impression of God. Small children assume that their parents know everything and perhaps even can do everything. So if children have questions, they assume their parents can answer them. The fact that the parents give an answer may be as important as the answer the parents give. Almost any answer is better than no answer. To tell the child, as we sometimes must, that we do not know, is difficult for the child to understand. If father and mother don't know, then who does? God? But for the child, who is God apart from parents?

The child's identification of parents with God is, of course, strained a bit when parents acknowledge that they do not know all the answers and that there are some things they cannot do. This identification gradually becomes modified—and needs to be—as the child develops. This gradual differentiation between parents and God is one of the characteristics of growing up. Some may acknowledge it intellectually, however, and still identify parents and God emotionally. One can also differentiate emotionally.

One of the purposes of adolescence is to learn to differentiate between God and parents. Is the resistance and even rebellion against parents during the teen years also a resistance and rebellion against God? Can an adolescent come to know this differentiation emotionally as well as intellectually? This is a major key to becoming one's own person, to becoming an adult. So how can parents work with their adolescent children toward this end? How can parents avoid becoming obstacles to their children's emotional maturation and freedom to grow up?

Nowhere is this more true than in the early stages when children begin to assert their will. This adolescent rebellion comes as a shock. This period is preceded by a period of relatively easy parenthood, called the plateau years. At the onset of adolescence children may seem to be betraying their parents. Children may become physically superior to parents and have growing knowledge and language skills. No longer may parents delight in being challenged. Parents remember well their own adolescent rebellion, and now there are threatened parents as well as threatened children. What if we parents cannot control these "strangers"?

If we are not careful, fear can take over, and we may react emotionally, just as adolescents do. Instead of seeing this period as important and necessary in a child's life, we can become immobilized, afraid that we are not up to the challenge. Yet the time for adolescents to distance themselves from us is now!

Some cultures, like that of the Hutterites, are wise enough to build in the expectation that their children will rebel, and they are healthier for it. Other groups remain rigid and expect teenagers to remain obedient children. Our culture gives children mixed messages in this matter. We want them to become mature, but we expect them to reach this maturity without experiencing conflict with their parents and working through these conflicts.

Because our goal is to produce adults who are responsible, habilitated contributing members of society, we need to appreciate and encourage independent thinking. We can help our adolescents learn acceptable ways to present *their* ideas by speaking clearly about *our* ideas. If we can keep our exchanges with our adolescents from becoming shouting matches, all of us can learn.

▼

The attitude that gains respect is one that takes into consideration the other's feelings and concerns.

Whenever one person expresses an opinion, it is not unusual for someone else to hear it as a challenge. Caving in to flawed logic and confused facts will produce no learning experiences for the adolescent. On the other hand, when adults expect obedience and respect on the basis of authority alone, they will probably get neither. The attitude that gains respect is one that takes into consideration the other's feelings and concerns. This kind of respect humanizes the parent-adolescent exchange and can prevent the all-too-familiar stalemate in communication. Then the wonderful growth inherent in the adolescent stage will be allowed to happen, and parents will have the privilege of knowing the unique person their adolescent is becoming.

One way we can help our children's maturation, even in the difficult times of adolescence, is to work at accepting our own limitations. Because we are not gods, there is no real pressure to have to cover our shortcomings, inadequacies, mistakes, stupidities, and even sins. Admitting our faults helps the child to differentiate emotionally between his or her parents and God. If this openness about our vulnerability can begin when our children are young, so much the better.

Journalist Bill Farmer[1] marvelously illustrates parental vulnerability. "Unadulterated joy," says Farmer, "comes to a child from watching father knock over a glass of milk at the dinner table." At first there is just the barely audible test laugh, and then the sniggles spread. Father is the one who did it! The children know what would happen if one of them had done it. "Father would glower, furrow his brow and in a pinched-mouthed understatement of contemptuous reserve, say, 'Well, just don't sit there—wipe it up!' Finally the snigglings break loose, and a voice cries out with unencumbered mirth. 'Daddy, *you* spilled the milk.'"

By now there is open laughter and even napkin throwing as one of the junior revolutionaries mimics, "Well, don't just sit there—wipe it up!" By now, says Farmer, the children are rolling on the floor.

Farmer goes on to say that he feels sorry for children whose father has never spilled the milk. He says you can spot them as adults with their sour faces and suspiciously darting eyes—anything but free spirits. But when Father spills the milk, he becomes "human and frail and fumbling and humble to the point of winning his children's compassion."

If you are the father or mother who spilled the milk, what would you do? Would you join in the fun and enjoy a healthy laugh at yourself with the children? Or would you get tight inside and put up with the shenanigans for a moment and then say something like, "OK, you've had your fun—let's get back to eating your supper"? Or why not join in the fun and roll on the floor with them?

Dealing with Defensiveness

Becoming a parent is an invitation to be vulnerable. This, however, is not the state of affairs most of us wish for ourselves. We would rather have an answer to every situation and present an aura of control, but by concealing our vulnerability from our children, we deprive them of the opportunity of getting to know us.

These feelings of vulnerability are often déjà-vu; we may react instinctively as we did when we were children as our own children trigger old memories. At various times in our parenting, our children can suddenly remind us of someone in our past. We may even call our child by the name of one of our siblings. Our childlikeness is brought to the surface by our child's childlikeness. If we are shamed by the child, we emotionally go back to a time when we were shamed as a child.

I (Lucy) remember reacting far more than necessary when one of my children said to me, "I wish I had Jean's mother instead of you." I am very vulnerable to being shamed. For a moment I was my child's age being told that I had not performed well. I imagine my child was confused by my overreaction.

Yet in a social outing, another child, tired of waiting, assigned the fault to me, saying, "I hate you!" and I was able placidly to reply, "I'm sure you do right now." Because the fault was not mine, I was not hooked. Knowing I was not to blame defused an otherwise negative reaction. Those particular words "I hate you" seemed at the moment to be therapeutic. The other family who actually caused the delay felt enraged by the child's comment. The father said, "I don't see how you can allow a child to say that to you. I'd slap any child of mine who said that!" They were unaware of their vulnerability and defensiveness.

As parents, our level of insecurity has much to do with our feeling of vulnerability when our children challenge us. I (Lucy) found that my own ego was very involved in childrearing. I was a "career" mother whose self-image was firmly tied to being a good mother. Any implication that I was doing less than very well was painful to me. Later I gained insight into these matters through workshops, seminars, and reading, but such opportunities were not available before and would have been very helpful earlier. Anyone can profit by becoming aware of his or her vulnerable spots. When we are unaware of our own vulnerability, we react emotionally to settle accounts and may displace our feelings onto a substitute target. Then we may simply act irrationally, become defensive, and do little or no listening.

Many of us have times when we respond by speaking first and listening later, if at all. I (Lucy) am exceedingly sensitive to criticism. As the youngest of six children, I felt unable to hold my own verbally or physically and felt inadequate and angry when I was criticized or when criticism was even implied. I felt something terrible would happen if I failed. So criticism become more of an issue than it needed to be.

When I am defensive and not aware of it, I do not draw others out. When my child wanted to trade me in for another mother, I would have learned so much if I had been able to say calmly, "What does Jean's mother do that I don't?" The answer might have ended the affair and I might have learned something. I prolonged it by my anger over my vulnerability.

Bill, on the other hand, is an oldest child. To him criticism was something that he was spared and consequently he believed it should not be part of his life. He says he defends himself rather than accepting the criticism, and because he is so intensely involved in defending himself, he also often does not listen.

When we find ourselves getting annoyed and wanting "to settle things in a hurry," it is a signal to slow down, ask clarifying questions, and try to disengage our emotions. At a workshop, human potentialist Syd Simon directed the participants to ask themselves the question, "What do I know that I don't want to know?" This exercise can be very helpful in clarifying where we are most vulnerable and most defensive.

Children need a certain stage of maturity to leave father and mother, but maturity is a lifelong growth process. Parents, too, need to mature. Even though we still feel defensive emotions, we can learn to resist the defensive reaction patterns of behavior that we so easily fall into. If you have any trouble identifying how you react when you are defensive with your children, ask your spouse or your children. Most of us, however, are quite well aware of how we react, and often it is the same way in which one of our parents reacted to us as children when they were defensive.

We need to begin first by changing our behavior. Usually feelings change after our behavior changes. There is an emotional time lag, but our emotions will eventually catch up to our behavior as we persist in doing things differently. While we cannot control or change our feelings to any great extent, we can control and change our behavior. This is particularly true if we perceive that God is calling us to parent differently. If we become aware of what our defensive reactions are, we can stop them and start over. As we do this more and more, the new patterns will become stronger, and the old defensive ones will lose their appeal.

While we are learning to curb our defensive reactions to some extent and to let ourselves be vulnerable before our children, they can be learning about unconditional love—agape love. Agape love is the love that God gives to us without any qualifications, unconditionally. We are loved as we are. As parents, we want to be loved for our good qualities, particularly by our children. But their greater challenge is to love us apart from our good qualities—in our flawed and faulty selves. Their opportunity to give us this kind of love makes our relationship with them more open and free. They can differ with us then in their adolescence and adulthood without unresolvable guilt, and the relationship itself is able to endure wider fluctuations and more risky exchanges. As Job could quarrel with God without endangering his relationship with God, so also conflicts and quarrels in our own families do not need to jeopardize relationships that are united by unconditional love and in which forgiveness is always available.

When Vulnerability Reverses the Roles

Much as we need our children to see us as vulnerable, there are circumstances in which a parent's vulnerability may become too much for children of any age. When parents experience severe grief, long-term illness, depression, unemployment, separation from mates, or sudden poverty, children may try to parent their parents. It is natural for children to try to provide the strength that they see as lacking. But in so doing they are likely to miss out on some of their own developmental needs.

For example, when there is grief over a death in the family—perhaps of a grandparent or even a child—the children may have nowhere to turn. Their own grief may be great, but often they have no one to hear them. Attention focuses on the grieving parent or parents. A well-meaning relative or friend of the family may say to the child or adolescent, "Your mother (father) is under a great strain. You must do all you can to help her (him)." This is asking too much of any child, but the child is likely to feel the responsibility and will try to find ways to help. Theresa Huntley's *Helping Children Grieve* (Minneapolis: Augsburg, 1991) is an excellent resource that offers suggestions for parents and other caring adults to help children grieve the loss of someone they love. Another is Edgar Jackson's *Telling a Child About Death* (New York: Channel Press, 1965).

In a time of grief or other vulnerability, the child's own development is put on hold. Adolescents in this situation may not express rebellion or be able to work through conflicts with the parents. In their perception, their parents are far too stressed to be able to cope with their children's rebellion. As adults they may carry a nebulous feeling of sadness. Later in life they may realize that their own problems and feelings were not dealt with and that they need to seek help. One of my (Bill's) counselees was in this situation and described her awareness of this by saying, "I'm tired of being the shoulder." At the time, however, taking care of the parent becomes so absorbing that the child's own emotions are shut down.

▼

Much as we need our children to see us as vulnerable, there are circumstances in which a parent's vulnerability may become too much for children of any age.

We experienced the death of our oldest child, Sally, when she was twenty-five. At first Bill was inconsolable even around the children. Our oldest son took him to task. "Stop it," he said. "You are upsetting the children." After that we tried to separate our need to grieve and our children's need to live a normal life. Only time will tell how well we did. A counselor friend reminded us that the effects of such a trauma can surface at any time in life.

The tension a single parent experiences can create similar pressures on children. Some children may think they have to make up for the companionship of the missing parent. Though they are missing the help of a partner, single parents we know realize that their children cannot replace the absent adult. These single parents often take advantage of support groups provided by churches and by community agencies that provide the specific help they need for their particular situation.

A friend of ours describes how she became parent to her parents years ago. During the great depression her family went from living comfortably to living in poverty. Her parents were traumatized. They could talk of nothing but their losses. Although she was just entering her teen years, she became the strong one in the family, assuring them that they could cope. Trying to parent her parents not only took away her natural time to rebel but also left her with a deep insecurity about money. Although she has always had plenty of money, it is never sufficient to allay her anxiety.

When the parents become vulnerable and the children begin to show signs of stress, the church can be a good resource for help. Each parish can identify persons, male and female, trained for counseling children, and can help in the referral. Children who carry their parents' problem often show this burden in negative behavior or depression. Today, teachers and other childcare providers are better prepared to recognize symptoms of unresolved problems. Such problems can affect the development of a child's faith. In suffering loss children may wonder whether God even exists, because their prayers were not answered. Their trust needs to be restored.

When life gets very heavy and seems to be more than we can cope with, we need to turn to God, our Heavenly Parent, rather than to our children for strength to carry on. This is particularly the case when unresolved marital conflicts eat away at our confidence and morale. Here again parents can look to the church. Your pastor or other counselor can help you with your heavy load without making it his or hers. The spiritual guidance you receive can help you to develop the habits of prayer and meditation that will support your trust in God. In this way you can find relief for your anxieties and give your children what Rabbi Edwin Friedman[2] calls a "nonanxious presence" that does so much for the health of family relationships.

▼

Things to Talk About and Do

1.   How did you feel about the power your parents had over you? Did they use it wisely?

2.   How does it feel when your children find out that you "spilled the milk," when you made a mistake or did something wrong? What is your reaction to them?

3.   On a sheet of paper, write answers to these questions. Don't rush. Take several minutes for each.

    a.   What situations make me defensive (anywhere, not just with my family)?

    b.   What situations make me feel vulnerable?

    c.   How do my children make me feel vulnerable?

Look over your responses. Do they have anything to do with your childhood home? Do you ever sound the way your parents sounded to you? Is any of this defensiveness unfinished business?

▼

Notes

1.   Bill Farmer, "When Father Spills the Milk," *St. Paul Pioneer Press,* 18 Sept. 1977, Focus, p. 3.

2.   Edwin Friedman, *From Generation to Generation* (New York: The Guilford Press, 1985).

▼▼▼

5

Developing Our Significant Relationships

▲▲

The toughest time in a marriage can be the childrearing years. The partnership in parenting can drain energy from the partnership in marriage. Being parents can take the focus from being married. The companionship dimension of marriage can disappear. Some people even conclude that children are not good for marriage.

A more positive approach would be to focus on how to keep parenting from being hard on the marriage. Fathers and mothers are doing their children a favor when they cultivate their marriage. The security of a good marriage provides security for the children. We recommend a weekly date night just to enjoy the relationship. It is also good to take a few days, annually or semiannually, to get away for a mini-vacation. This may require money for sitters but it is a good investment. In the later years of marriage, adult children can be a blessing to the marriage even though the children may not have been viewed that way during the childrearing years.

Denying Our Personal Needs

Some parents tend to deny their own needs for their children. Is this a parental instinct? Or is it a sense of parental obligation? Such parental sacrificing may present no major problem, except that we parents can be double-minded over which sacrifices to make. This double-mindedness is shown in our resentment later if such sacrifices have not "paid off." Two payoffs come to mind. The first is that our children should fulfill the mental pictures we have for them—that they live up to our expectations. The second is that they show they are grateful for our sacrifices, probably by telling us occasionally what great parents we have been. But what if one or both of these do not come about?

Some women tend to deny their needs for the sake of their children and then use such sacrifices as good excuses for not developing their own personal potential. Men—under less pressure in our society to be good parents until recently—tend to deny their needs for peace in the marriage. This is particularly true if their jobs are demanding. They need peace at home and may deny their personal needs to have that peace so that they can devote their energy to their jobs. Such men are also cheating on their own development as persons because their imbalanced lives sooner or later fail to provide the satisfaction necessary for their personal fulfillment.

Women who have careers in addition to their homemaking still continue to deny their needs for their children. The woman is often considered to be the primary caregiver of the home. Also, her investment in the child through pregnancy and nursing creates a bond that fathers find more difficult to attain. For whatever reason a parent may sacrifice his or her own needs for the family, the result can be a loss in developing one's own relationship with oneself.

Relating to Ourselves

Another relationship beside our relationship to our spouse and children deserves attention, and that is our relationship to ourselves. Being a person means being in a relationship. I relate to me—and it is not always a good relationship. I may treat myself worse than I treat others, or less graciously. As my spouse has needs, our marriage has needs, our children have needs, and our parent-child relationships have needs, so also my relationship with me has needs. In the midst of our childrearing years we should meet our needs as persons and also as married persons. We need to find ways to meet our own needs in order to develop confidence in ourselves and to experience joy in living.

A notable side effect to taking care of ourselves and our marriage during the childrearing years is that it is good for our children. Writing on family life, Quaker educator Elton Trueblood and his wife Pauline say this about parental self-fulfillment: "More good is done for children by the parents' habit of happiness than by their obvious deeds of sacrifice."[1] Our *being* is basic to our *doing* and so we need to nurture our being.

Taking care of ourselves not only has many advantages, it is also a Christian response. It is within our calling as God's people to meet our own needs but not at the expense of others. At times we are called to set aside our needs, to deny ourselves, to care for the needs of others. We may wonder whether such sacrificing of our needs is detrimental to our own self-development. To find out, we need to ask why we are doing it. If we are primarily satisfying our conscience so that we will not feel guilty, then we may resent the sacrifice. The double-mindedness behind such guilt-oriented choices ultimately takes its toll.

But if our decision to sacrifice is based on our own sense of values, priorities, and commitment, we have made an integrated choice to deny ourselves. Although the choice is one of self-denial, it is also self-fulfilling. We feel good about making the choice because it is in line with our calling, our identity. It is a *gospel* choice. But if our sacrifice is primarily a *law* choice, a choice determined by oughts or musts or shoulds, then we may feel resentment and think that our children or others owe us something.

A mother of a Girl Scout who wanted to help with the volunteer services to her children illustrates how recognizing and accepting her individuality led her to self-fulfillment. Long before denim became fashionable she wore it and she also had a no-care hairstyle. "I am an artist," she said. "If I give that up, I will resent the demands on me. I want to help, but my home will not look like the furniture ads, and my children will not be able to bring home-baked treats, but I will do whatever else you think will help."

A Model for Loving Others

A scribe who had listened to Jesus answer many questions was impressed. He saw his chance to ask something he had been pondering: "Which commandment is the first of all?" Jesus answered, "The first is, 'Hear O Israel: the Lord our God, the Lord is one; you shall love the Lord your God with all your heart, and with all your soul, and with all your mind, and with all your strength.' The second is this, 'You shall love your neighbor as yourself.' There is no other commandment greater than these" (Mark 12:29-31).

It is the second of these commandments that concerns us here. The love that we are to give to God is the same love (agape) that we are to give to our neighbor (spouse, children, parents, others). This love that we give to our neighbor is modeled after the love that we give ourselves. First John 4:19 says, "We love because God first loved us." Here is where it all begins. We love ourselves, our neighbor, and our God because we first received God's love in Christ.

Unconditional love (agape) is a self-giving, noncalculating love that, after we have received it, we can give. As God accepts, so we can accept. As God is kind, so we can be kind. As God is patient, so we can be patient. As God cares, so we can care. We show this kind of love to ourselves, which then in turn serves as a model and guide for loving others—our children, our spouse, our parents, our neighbors, everyone.

It is our love for ourselves and thereby for others that helps us decide moment by moment whether to deny our needs for the sake of others and ourselves, or to fulfill our needs for the sake of ourselves and others. We care for ourselves for others' sake as well as our own. God's love combines all other loves, so that in loving myself and others, I am responding to the call of God to take care of the gifts that God's love has given.

Our Faith Centers in Relationships

Our Christian faith centers in relationships. The good news of forgiveness and reconciliation gives our relationships the security that they need both to endure and to develop. The relationship that God establishes with us through God's overture of reconciling love, beside being a relationship in and of itself, also is realized in our relationship with others, especially our relationships with our children.

During her adolescence one of our daughters "fell out of love" with me (Bill). This was hard for me to take because we had been quite close. The counselor I consulted perceived my anxiety and offered me this counsel: "Don't read foreverness into this present moment." It was what I needed to hear. We worry that when our family relationships become troubled, they will stay troubled. Belief in the God who stays with us through these ups and downs in our family relationships can break this sense of doom by giving us hope. Søren Kierkegaard defines faith in God as believing that with God all things are possible. Therefore change is possible. It was this faith that helped me to follow the counsel of my counselor. I could hope for change because my relationship with my daughter was inextricably combined with my relationship with God.

The hope inherent in our faith can prevent us from overreacting in our difficulties with our children. In the psalmist's words, we can "wait on the Lord" (Ps. 27:14) instead of reading foreverness into our difficulties. The light touch of parents who wait and hope is healthier for children than the heaviness of the overreacter. We who hope believe that more options are available for our children and for us than we are aware of in our anxious moments. The nonanxious, nonreactive approach of a parent who believes in the God of hope is precisely what a child needs in his or her own anxious moments.

Growing to Appreciate Our Relationships

Sometimes it takes a trauma for us to realize how central our relationships are to our own fulfillment. A good friend of ours went through major surgery to save his life. It was a debilitating shock to his body and it took him a long time to recuperate. In spite of this he said to me, "I thank God for this whole traumatic experience." Because he is not the kind of person one would expect to say such a thing, I asked him to explain. "I have been deeply impressed during this time of my illness by my wife's love for me. I never really perceived it in such magnitude before. My greater appreciation of our relationship has made the illness worth it." Theologically I would not say that God willed his illness. But I can say that God used it—greatly.

Traumas like our friend's help us to get beyond the game-playing stage in our significant relationships. (By significant relationships we mean family relationships: our relationship with our spouse, children, parents, and siblings, plus our relationship with ourselves and with God—all of these may be critically significant for our parenting.) Traumas open us to the movement of growth in these relationships, to the resolution of conflict, and to our own ability to receive the love that is offered. Of course, in our finite and flawed human condition, we can regress as well as progress in our relationships. But if we can accept such regressions and use them as a way of gaining deeper insight into ourselves, they will help us further in our relationships.

One of the things we can do to strengthen our relationships with our children is to examine the possible obstacles in our relationship with our own parents. Again our relationship with God gives us the hope and courage to take the initiative to examine and discover the strengths and weaknesses of those relationships.

Mark, for example, made this effort even before he became a parent because he believed his reluctance to become a parent was tied to the poor relationship he had with his own parents. His parents were divorced when he was a teenager, which had much to do with his uncomfortable relationship with them.

So after much prayer, Mark decided to talk with his father first, probably because he felt a bit more at ease with him. During the first talk, Mark was able to get past some of his father's defensiveness so that both were able to share their hurts.

▼

The hope inherent in our faith can prevent us from overreacting in our difficulties with our children.

The conversation with his mother was more difficult because she interpreted his initiative as judgment on her parenting. Her tears would have made him abandon the effort if he had not believed that God had directed him. He still hoped for change. After several visits, his mother finally saw that Mark was more interested in loving her than in putting her down. Within a few months, Mark reached the place where he felt comfortable in the presence of both parents. As a by-product of his efforts, he saw what he had not seen before—that his parents really cared for him and were proud of him.

Mark was exhilarated when his efforts paid off in an improved relationship with his parents. As an adult son, he can now look forward to a growing relationship with parents who have also now become his friends. Taking care of unfinished business from his childhood has prepared the way for unencumbered relationships with any children he himself may have.

If one or both of your parents are no longer living or otherwise not available, you can achieve much of this clearing of obstacles by going to a counselor, letting the counselor take the role of your parent and talking with him or her. It may even be wise to seek counseling first before you take the initiative with your living parents. You will have the opportunity, then, to rid yourself of any double-mindedness that you may have regarding the visit, as well as any latent bad feelings that still may be lingering in your memories. Also, pray about the visit—that God will keep both you and your parent open to God's guidance.

When the time comes, remind yourself to be patient. Your parents may well be resistant and defensive, perhaps even denying that any problem exists. They may instinctively feel unwelcome guilt and see your approach as an attack. So give them time to express this resistance without pushing too hard. Simply restate your feelings and your desire to improve the relationship.

The chances are good that after a while the defenses will come down and your parent will hear you. This is also a time for *you* to hear. Both of you can receive and learn from each other. As in Mark's case, it may take more than one session to accomplish this. Whatever progress you make will not only be helpful for your own parenting, but it will also open new possibilities for growth in your relationship with your parents. You may actually come to enjoy each other more and be able to share more. Keep yourself open to this possibility.

Respecting Our Children's Relationships

This same kind of learning through experience applies to our children's relationships as well. They need a certain amount of freedom to choose friends and to decide their degree of closeness to family members. They will profit from parental guidance in these relationships, but not from parental manipulation. Children can be quite adept at manipulating (particularly their parents) without any modeling from us. They may find it hard not to exploit differences they perceive between Mom and Dad when they see the advantages. This is particularly true during times of marital conflict, separation, or divorce. Each child has his or her relationship with each parent and may feel more positive toward the one parent—the mother, for example—than the other. This may be difficult for that parent, who at least subconsciously might find satisfaction if the child had felt similar resentments. If this happens to us, we need to resist the temptation to "set the child straight." Each relationship has its own unique story. We can trust our children's own ability to assess their relationship with our estranged partner. Even if the marriage is healthy, each child needs to relate directly with each parent without the other parent running interference.

This same kind of noninterference is needed in children's relationships with their grandparents. I (Bill) experienced a tension in this regard because I wanted both my parents and our children to like each other. They saw their grandparents only on semiannual visits, and so I found myself putting pressure on this or that child to reduce any tension with their grandparents. Now I realize that they needed to work out their own relationships with the grandparents. Any tensions were the grandparents' challenge, not mine as a parent. Later one of our daughters as a teenager had a way of needling her elderly grandfather. I realized even then that he needed this stimulation—it "kept his juices going."

The same is true with children's relationships with each other. Sibling rivalries and conflicts are nothing new. Spacing in the family, genetic differences, environmental differences, and the comparisons others make all contribute to the problem. No wonder siblings quarrel and fight! But it is hard for parents to endure this. Your family may be in the midst of such fighting now. Let us assure you, things can change. Our two youngest children had a period of intense feuding, even physical fighting. Today as young adults they are best of friends.

A TV station conducted an experiment in which by random phoning they offered families a certain amount of money to turn off their TV sets for a month. Those who agreed had the sets removed by a television repairman who observed that removing the set was like a "death in the family."

Amazingly TV plays a role in children's quarreling. This experiment and others show that children fight much more without the TV to distract them. But they also show that these same children were better able to work through their quarrels to a resolution—when there was no TV to distract them.

Children need help from their parents in their conflicts with each other. They should not be permitted to be destructive. I (Bill) know from my experience as a pastoral counselor the damage siblings can do to each other of which their parents are not aware. Older siblings have exploited, terrorized, and molested younger ones. Younger ones can exploit their "littleness" to get the parents on their side. As parents we should remain vigilant and always give such behavior our full attention. At least we can raise questions so that we are more alert to the clues. We parents need to remain the parents. This means we do not delegate parental responsibilities to older siblings. Not only may they resent these responsibilities, but they are not ready for them. It is not fair to either the older or the younger siblings. Of course they can learn under parental guidance to take some responsibility for younger children, but this is something other than being substitute parents.

▼

We learn from our experiences, both the pleasant and the unpleasant, when we believe in the God who is greater than those experiences.

We can teach our children how to deal creatively with their conflicts. As parents, our own marriage can be a model for them. How do we deal with our conflicts, both in the children's presence and in private? We can acknowledge that conflict occurs in any good relationship. Working through it without physical or verbal violence can lead to closer intimacy. As husband and wife persist in the resolution of conflict until they reach some sort of understanding and follow this with the hugs and kisses of reconciliation, the children have been taught more than words alone can teach.

We learn from our experiences, both the pleasant and the unpleasant, when we believe in the God who is greater than those experiences. Our children need our help in reflecting on their conflicts with siblings as well as with neighborhood and school friends and foes. We can work with them to discover ways of coping and problem solving that build rather than undermine their self-esteem. We can help them see that God is teaching them in all of their experiences.

Coping with Irritation

Despite all the wonderful things that can come to us through our significant relationships, irritations can make daily living difficult. The sources of irritation are sometimes almost impossible to trace and can be irrational. For example, I (Bill) am irrationally irritated when members of the family chew gum. This has caused many unnecessary conflicts in our home. Realizing that the sound of gum chewing cannot really cause pain unless I allow it, I decided that the way to overcome this irritation was to chew gum myself. Now when I do, others complain that I chew too loudly.

Producing strong yet cooperative individuals is the family's challenge. Our own preferred individual ways of being and doing may irritate those who must live closely with us. Children irritate parents. Parents annoy children. Do you find your children inexplicably irritating you? And have you not felt your child's irritation at you? All of us would like to live with a minimum of irritations. What a stress reducer that would be!

Because parents are supposedly more mature (even though they may return to childish ways when irritated), they are the ones to recognize and deal with irritation. Chapter 13 of 1 Corinthians, often called the love chapter, is also about irritation. Love, it says, is not easily irritated, not easily provoked (13:5). *The Interpreter's Bible* comments on this verse, "Love can be angry but not irritated." Anger has to do with injustice, but irritation has to do with annoyance. In our insecurity, we parents do sometimes take offense.

Some children seem always to demand more than necessary. Why is that so? New parents sometimes are confused about answering their child's demands. They might feel uncomfortable and insecure if they do not meet every demand, and yet they know that somewhere discipline for the child must begin. The demands may be as simple as asking for an ice cream cone or extra time before bed. Those childhood manipulations, if not resisted, can sow the seed for later adolescent conflicts.

If we know ourselves and our unmet needs well, we can prevent some adolescent tugs-of-war over such things as who can have the car. Parents sometimes deny privileges or give unwise ones on the basis of their own life experience rather than on the maturity of the child or the situation at hand.

Our guilt feelings over these irritations only complicate the resolution of the issues. Because we live in a covenant of forgiveness, the guilt is removed, and parents are able to analyze and recognize what is causing the irritation and work toward coming to peace with it. There is no contradiction between accepting our children as they are and holding firm to the standards we believe they should follow. Our needs and those of our children can coexist, showing them that the world can be a friendly place even when we don't always get what we want.

We often respond to irritation by overcorrecting our children. In the letter to the Colossians the admonishment to children to obey parents (3:20) is balanced with the more difficult directive; fathers are warned against provoking (or overcorrecting: 3:21 KJV) their children. According to *The Interpreter's Bible,* provoking is like "chafing" or letting your children know that they can never do anything right, which is exactly the feeling produced by prolonged irritation. We live within the tension between correcting and overcorrecting. Even adult children may take offense at any hint of disapproval from their parents. Even with all the help of psychologists, pastors, and other helping professionals, we can still feel insecure in our judgment and for good reason. Parenting is not an exact science. Correcting our children is our duty, but to sully our authority by destroying self-esteem is another matter.

Our insecurity is often the instigator of overcorrection. In our defensiveness we may strike out before we use our cognitive reasoning. When we become aware of the choices we have at any time, we remember that we can take the forgiveness God offers and start over.

Knowing the Shadow

Authorities offer many explanations of our unintended reactions. One of these is what Carl Jung called the "shadow," (see chapter 3). William Miller's book, *Making Friends with your Shadow,* builds on this concept in a practical way. Miller helps us to recognize our dark impulsive side, which often seeks to harm others. It is possible in moments of irritation that parents can wish to hurt their children. We need to be confronted. One of the best ways to do this is to raise questions. I (Bill) have felt fortunate that people have confronted me when I showed irritation with a child. I remember well the time when our small son said to me after I had spanked his sister, "Why are you so mean to her?" It was an eye-opener. We also know what does not work when a parent needs to be confronted: indirect slams or blanket accusations such as "You never speak well of Joan," or "Why is such a little thing bothering you?" As a spouse, we can be both brave and gentle if we see children being hurt. Sometimes a mother is allowed to continue reacting in a way that hurts a child because she is considered too distraught and overwhelmed. A father may be allowed to continue in irritable behavior because everyone knows his work is so stressful. These are times when it is difficult to recognize our shadow's influence in our relationship with our children. But through prayer and candid conversation with our partner and others who may be supportive to us, insights can be found.

▼

When we become aware of the choices we have at any time, we remember that we can take the forgiveness God offers and start over.

Can we listen to the brave questions? Am I acting on feelings that I cannot account for?

Do you ever feel that "yes" is the answer? We surely do, and even though our opportunity to explore these feelings came after our children had matured, it was most helpful. The willingness to be humble and to be challenged is part of our Christian heritage. Being an authority in any situation does not mean that I can't say, "I was wrong." Real authority can say, "I see where I may have been wrong. What can I do now to restore myself?"

Some of the most fulfilling times in my life have been when I (Bill) have been able to talk to my children about situations in which I felt guilty for having "provoked" them as children (amazingly, they don't even seem to remember). I overreacted when I was irritated. Such meetings with our children are not easy, but if we believe in confession and forgiveness, we can do it. Today with many church organizations sponsoring Christian growth seminars and with so many books on the subject of knowing ourselves, most of us have an opportunity to learn and to grow.

Sometimes our irritation is really an excuse to find a scapegoat. On a walking trip of England, I (Lucy) became aware that our leader, not a sensitive man, was scapegoating the two youngest members of our group. He focused on their lack of participation in meal preparation. I had experience with people their age and saw that the problem was that they were being shut out by other efficient members of the group. They were not strong enough to challenge him and were probably more confused than angry by his hurtful, critical remarks. I asked them to help prepare the vegetables and they soon were functioning well. They were neither lazy nor incompetent. Others can often intervene in such a situation while neither the person who scapegoats nor the person receiving the destructive messages can. Being timid when one could do something helps no one. The responsibility for taking action falls to each of us according to our gifts and understanding.

Recognizing Differing Personalities

Children who are always easily managed may need to examine and express negative thoughts. For them, challenging authority seems impossible. In a family close to ours, I (Bill) observed that the elder son was treated differently from the younger one. To an outside observer, the elder son seemed capable of always pleasing his parents. The older, easily managed child, although conforming, really resented being used by his parents and eventually proved conclusively how much hatred he was feeling. When he became a young man, he sabotaged all the dreams his parents had for him.

So easily managed children may be at risk. If they gain and reinforce their position by pleasing others, they are missing the reality of conflict. Fear rather than feelings of love may be controlling their actions. Those who comply with authority often show a mean scapegoating streak which probably has its origin in unexpressed anger. Skillful counselors of youth groups may be the first to notice and to help the young person understand his or her conflicting behaviors.

While the child who is easily managed is less often perceived as needing help, the child who is really difficult to manage gives parents the most worry. Parents and educators working with such children often choose to give up. The father with the easily managed older son had a young son who constantly irritated him. The father was obviously uncomfortable in the younger son's presence. The battle of their wills was never resolved. The father was afraid to deal with his own panic. He neither disciplined the boy nor approved of him. His irritation dominated the relationship.

Other parents may share this father's fear of disciplining. If one parent refuses to set limits, the other parent is placed at a disadvantage.

Do you ever ask the question, "Why do I have such a hard time being firm?"—if you do? Or "Why does a child's resistance to my request stir such vehement irritation?"—if it does?

Our children need us also to mature. They will become more self-confident when we adults react to them as persons who know where they want firmness, who do not overidentify with them but who want to connect with their need to become adults. The best way that a child can know how to be adult is to be with *real* adults.

Often difficulties in our relationships result from differences in personality types. The Myers-Briggs Type Indicator can be helpful in this area. It identifies each person's primary characteristics according to several categories, all of which have their advantages. After the inventory is scored by a testing service, a session is spent interpreting the results.

Both of our daughters took the test and the results surprised us as parents. It confirmed what they already knew but which we didn't. One of their qualities was that of an introvert. With both parents the opposite of her—extroverts—no wonder we were sometimes at odds.

One of the best evenings our family spent together was after we found that all of us had taken the Myers-Briggs. We compared our responses to the test with each other and explored the effect our personality types had upon our relationships. The test did us a great favor by giving us the language and support for such a discussion. Nothing has emphasized more for us the positive contribution that all traits can make. All are equally acceptable in spite of any cultural biases. We wish we had had this material available to us when our children were adolescents.

An excellent resource for learning more about the Myers-Briggs Type Indicator is *God's Gifted People* by Gary Harbaugh (Minneapolis: Augsburg, 1990). The author gives examples of questions to give readers some clues about their personality type before they contact a counseling center or testing service to take the long version of the test. The book gives helpful information on interpreting and appreciating the various characteristics and on living and working together with our differences.

▼

Things To Talk About and Do

1. What obstacles have you had or do you have in your relationship with your parents? How do those problems affect your relationship with your children?

2. Think of examples when you have set aside your needs for the sake of your children.

    a. When did you feel good about doing so? Why?

    b. When did you feel resentful? Why?

3. Think of examples when you chose *not* to set aside your needs. How did you feel? Why?

4. How does focusing on the uniqueness of each child help you accept that child? How are your children different from each other? In your childhood home, how were you different from your brothers or sisters?

▼

Note

1. Elton and Pauline Trueblood, *Recovery of Family Life* (New York: Harper, 1953), 74.

6

Helping Our Children Feel Good About Their Sexuality

The founder of Logotherapy, Victor Frankl, said that in observing the American scene he was convinced that our preoccupation with sex is due in part to our loss of a spiritual sense of meaning in our lives. Sex, specifically orgasm, has been substituted to fill the vacuum. But, he said, sex really cannot fill the vacuum and will finally let us down. We can express our sense of meaning and purpose through sex, but we cannot find it there.

As God created us, sexual intercourse was given to us not only as a way of reproduction, but as a celebration of committed love. Sex therefore is a primary means of expressing love and affection. Unfortunately in our fallenness, this same capacity can be distorted into expressing hate.

A Distinctively Human Sexuality

God created us as sexual beings—"male and female he created them" (Gen. 1:27). Our sexual nature gives us one way of reaching out affectionately to others. Usually this attraction to others develops a particular focus on the opposite sex during the years of puberty. Sex, as God created it, is a physical expression of the spiritual—a bodily communication of the warmth of love. "Have you hugged your child today?" says a bumper sticker. In terms of Christian theology we could say, "Have you *incarnated* your love to your child today?" That is, have you given some bodily form to your love? Have you given it the tangible touch that it needs?

79

Sex is a bodily function but it centers in the mind and spirit. In our culture one of our favorite physical symbols of affection is the kiss. It also was a favorite in the fellowship of the early church. In four of his letters, St. Paul encourages the congregation to greet each other with a holy kiss (Rom. 16:16; 1 Cor. 10:20; 2 Cor. 13:12; 1 Thess. 5:26). A *holy* kiss is one "set apart" for the sisters and brothers in the family of God as a way of expressing their love for each other without implying sexual attraction. St. Peter describes the same symbol as a "kiss of love [agape]" (1 Pet. 5:14). In a story from Luke's Gospel, a woman of the street came into the house where Jesus was eating and poured expensive ointment on his feet, dried them with her hair and kissed them. (Luke 7:36-48). Jesus said that this was her way of showing her love for the forgiveness she had received.

But there is also the dark side—the perverted use of this symbol. When Judas arranged to betray Jesus, the sign by which he would identify Jesus to the arresting soldiers was that he would kiss him. And when he did, Jesus said to him, "Judas, is it with a kiss that you are betraying the Son of Man?" (Luke 22:48).

The biblical term for having sexual intercourse is to "know" as in Genesis 4:1: "Now the man knew his wife Eve, and she conceived and bore Cain." This is no mere euphemism. In the physical joining of intercourse one "knows" the other. There is a coming together physically, mentally, and spiritually. The pleasure of sex is the pleasure of knowing another in such intimacy. The Christian principles governing sexual behavior develop from this understanding of sex. God designed them to enhance this pleasure of sex rather than to restrict it.

This distinctly human understanding of sex contrasts with that of the animal world. Animals are endowed by their creator with instincts that limit their sexual desire to times for reproduction. This instinct governs their sexual behavior.

In creating human beings in the creator's own image, God endowed us with the capacity to make decisions. We use our head in conjunction with our heart in determining our sexual behavior. For human beings sexual desire is one thing, sexual behavior another. Neither the desire nor the behavior need be related to times for reproduction. Nowhere is our human decision-making ability more needed than in our current attitudes toward sex. Movies, TV programs, books, magazines, and songs seem based on animal instinct rather than on the decision-making capacity of humans.

This distinctly human approach to sex began for most of us with our parents' marriage, which obviously was a sexual marriage. This is true even if we are adopted, because the environment in which we grow up influences our sexual understanding. Our earliest observations about sexuality ideally came from our parents' affection toward each other and toward us. Even if we didn't see much affection in our childhood home, we may have observed it in other families.

Nothing teaches like example. When our children watch married couples and notice their interaction, they are learning. A husband and wife who delight in each other cannot hide that fact. Children catch falseness very easily, but they also are able to tell which marriages are loving and healthy. If parents have friends who are especially happy together, it is good if the children can be around them. More important than talk, conferences, books, or media are good examples.

In one of our marriage enrichment workshops, a woman told about early memories of her mother sitting on her father's lap. This sight of affection between the parents was a positive influence in her attitude toward her own sexuality and her subsequent sexual relations with her husband. Even such a modest symbol as parents holding hands can communicate the warmth and healthiness of sexuality to children. Our sexual attractions and the feelings they engender have many of their roots in our mental images from our early childhood.

As a married couple, we can reinforce the values we hold by enjoying our own marriage and letting our children see that we enjoy it. We can affirm our Christian conviction that marriage is a good and honorable estate by respecting other people's marriages and marriage in general.

Using a Gospel Approach

Sexual energy can be compared to nuclear energy in that both can be used either constructively or destructively. Which way the power will be used depends on those who have the authority to make the decisions.

For nuclear power, it is those in authority in government; with sexual power, it is the authority of the individual.

What influences the decision maker? This question is the key to the ounce of prevention that is worth the pound of cure. Because early impressions are important, from the beginning we should use the gospel approach with our children—the good news that their sexual nature is God-given and therefore good. The law, rules, and regulations regarding sexual behavior are also good and, as mentioned earlier, are meant to enhance the pleasure of sex by preventing sex from becoming destructive. We need discipline in this area of our life as we do elsewhere. Discipline is the asset we develop that enables us to be in charge of ourselves, to direct our lives according to our beliefs, convictions, and inherent sense of "what is right." As we said earlier, discipline comes from the same root word as "disciple," which refers to learning. A disciple is a learner or follower, and discipline is putting this learning into practice.

> **Children need to know from the beginning that their sexuality is good, that their sexual curiosity is good, and that their desire for sexual pleasure is good.**

But laws and rules need to be preceded by the gospel for discipline to develop. It is the good news of unconditional love that gives to the self its foundation. Prior to "no, no" is "yes, yes." Prior to knowing what may be wrong about sexual behavior is knowing what is right about it. Children need to know from the beginning that their sexuality is good, that their sexual curiosity is good, and that their desire for sexual pleasure is good. Then they can be spared the unnecessary guilt about being sexual beings that undermines their discipline.

The first learning we receive is of the heart—the experience of being loved. Head learning is best when it is combined with heart learning. Sexual discipline, morality, and ethics are products of the personal security one receives from incarnational love, that is, love that is expressed tangibly. We can only genuinely follow morals and rules and laws when they are our own and not something imposed on us from without, against which we naturally rebel.

This incarnational love in which we receive the spiritual through the physical is epitomized in the person of Jesus, through whose humanity divinity is revealed. God chose to reveal God's nature through a human being so that human beings could understand in human, sensory terms who God is.

We receive this incarnational love sacramentally in the Lord's Supper in which the tangible elements of bread and wine communicate the intangible body and blood of Christ. The bread and wine are incarnational symbols in that they communicate what they symbolize. As the earthly elements enter the body, the heavenly elements nourish the spirit. In this sacramental understanding, participating in the Lord's Supper is like receiving the Lord's "touch." This touch—this incarnational expression of the spirit—communicates God's unconditional love. Similarly, parents' touch reflects this same love, providing the security and sense of belonging that children need in order to develop their identity as individuals with the authority to direct themselves.

Recognizing the Dark Side of Sex

But there is also a dark side of sex. Unfortunately in our fallenness the capacity for expressing sexual love as affection can be distorted. Sexual behaviors range all the way from the mutually satisfying celebration of love to the hate-filled violence of rape.

Children must learn to live in a fallen world. Not everybody is their friend. Children not only need to be wary of the approach of strangers but even of people they know. Most sexual molestation is done by friends and relatives of the children. As much as we dislike disturbing their sense of security and trust, we need to warn them because there are unhealthy people in our midst who may abuse them. We need to teach our children the difference between good touch and bad touch. Children need to know what strangers or "friends" ought not to be permitted to do to them. They also need our encouragement to tell us immediately if such incidents take place.

Too often children feel guilty after such an experience and are reluctant to let parents, teachers, or other trusted adults know. They may also have been threatened by the perpetrator. They need to know that *telling i*s the best thing to do and that they will be received positively when they do. They need to be reassured that no harm will come to them from telling, that parents can be trusted to protect them.

We need never apologize for protecting our children against bad touch. We must give clear guidelines with no chance for misinterpretation. Early conformity to rules of sexual conduct sets the stage for responsible adult behavior. Children should have all their questions about anatomy answered, and most of us are surprised to find out how few of these questions are sexual.

Christianity clearly teaches us to care for and respect our bodies. Sleeping and bathing separately from adults and children of the opposite sex is the beginning of learning privacy boundaries and individuality. This conduct needs to be done in a matter-of-fact, healthy way. The most important aspect is that it be followed consistently and that the rules must not be broken for emergencies. The beginning of incest or other abuse could occur from emergency sleeping or bathing arrangements. Children and adolescents do not have the necessary judgment to recognize danger.

Establishing Respect for Sexuality

As they grow, we may notice that our children's sexuality may differ from ours due to a combination of genetics, cultural influences, and peer pressure. When we are alert to our children's different rates of development and are willing to listen to their concerns, our children will sense that we understand them. If we do not always understand them, we can still respect them.

Perhaps the subject of sexuality is one in which grandparents, who are further removed from the ego struggles of parenting, can be wisely consulted. They may be able to point out family patterns over the generations. All of us who relate to the children can try to understand what is going on with them and offer them counsel, support, and love whenever we have the opportunity.

Preadolescent children need to learn about the changes that sexual maturation effects in their bodies. In our talks together, they can learn how their genetic makeup may affect their physical and emotional processes. We can also prepare them for changes to come. Both boys and girls need this information. Boys especially need to learn, within the family setting, that respect for the process of reproduction is part of becoming mature.

Ideally the family is a safe place to discuss and understand physical changes. When we speak of the process of reproduction in correct and respectful tones, we are helping to shape the attitudes our children will have when they are older. If, in separate male and female gatherings, sexual matters are talked about with disrespect and connected with violence, attitudes will not be challenged. However, the positive example of a man appreciating a woman's femininity and woman enjoying man's masculinity will help their children later establish the warmth needed for positive sexual contact which includes the mind and spirit.

▼

Boys especially need to learn, within the family setting, that respect for the process of reproduction is part of becoming mature.

A good way to help children understand that sexual activity is intended for marriage is to teach both sexes homemaking skills. These build confidence so that they will be able to share the workload equally with their spouse in their future home. "Who takes out the garbage?" is still a question that often defines role responsibility. A put-upon partner is not a good sexual partner. If one partner has all the authority in dividing the work responsibilities, something is wrong.

Opportunities for young people to learn adult roles are well handled in some classroom setting where they are taught the realities of parenthood by having to keep a chicken egg with them for a week. This egg always has to be in their care, or, if necessary, they may leave it in the care of a responsible person. This teaches that any activity, including sexual activity, involves responsibility. They learn about themselves and the nature of commitment for nurturing. Wise parents know that the skill of caring for and comforting children and babies is part of growing up. Classes offered by the YWCA and similar groups reinforce and measure these important skills and accomplishments and test this skill in an objective setting. Sex education includes basic facts, but also teaches caring and nurturing of children by both sexes. Sex should not be a selfish act, because it has infinite ramifications for both adults and children. Enjoying children and learning from watching them grow and play is an aspect of sex. Watching our children mature as sexual beings is as much a part of sexuality as is the sexual act itself.

The stability of our society depends on respect for the rules of sexual conduct. Societal breakdown occurs when reciprocal positive behavior and goodwill between the sexes cannot be counted on. People who want to ensure that their children will be able to grow up in a stable environment work diligently in their churches and communities. This work is often taken for granted and its pressure is seldom acknowledged. We get the impression from the media that sexuality has nothing to do with community nurturing or the provision of safety for those who cannot provide it for themselves. Children who learn that service and responsibility are connected with sex are on their way to responsible adulthood. From visiting many churches, we can see that this nurturing aspect of society is functioning much better than many people realize.

How the Media Manipulate Us

Although most children form healthy attitudes toward their bodies and sex, some are influenced by the presentation of sexual activity by the media. According to some estimates based on five hours of television viewing per day, adolescent boys and girls watch 1200 to 1500 sexual acts or references per year. The most common act portrayed was intercourse between unmarried people. Intercourse within marriage was second to last, just above rape.[1]

The media seem to have an agenda that we parents may wish to suppress. Erotic scenes exploit all of us. Adolescents who feel stirrings of their own potential for sexual activity find such movies, television, songs, and magazines especially appealing. The media seem to make liars out of adults who are counseling, "Wait."

Often violence is added to sex, which makes the image even more arousing for some people. Actually we might say it is destructive, because the explicit sexual representations on the screen are rarely associated with community. And even though they represent *some* reality, they are usually an appeal to the basest instincts of seduction and hurt. Because in general men are physically stronger than their women partners, the media often depict harm coming to women.

Neither boys nor girls derive any value from these pictures that seem to come complete with instructions on "how to do it" in illicit settings. The media glorify the strength of men over women and appeal to violence so much that men may not be able to react positively to a woman who shows strength and maturity.

When the father of a friend became disabled from heart disease, I (Lucy) had the opportunity to see that a man could remain a man although dependent on a woman. Their household functioned normally in spite of his dependency. Both partners in a marriage need to be able to be strong. The words "in sickness and health" from the marriage vows imply that we may need to adapt when situations change. Sexual expression in the time of financial or health reversals requires adjustments so that caring and understanding are lovingly communicated.

The media also falsely portray the consequences of pregnancy outside marriage. Unplanned pregnancies are often presented in an attractive manner, and AIDS or other sexually transmitted diseases are rarely part of the story. In real life, such an event usually destroys a woman's youth and limits her choices. While people may be able to adjust to the new situation, pregnancies outside of marriage are still unfortunate. We can be sympathetic to unwed fathers, but it is still the woman and her family who have to make the most adjustments. The woman's parents are called on to be supportive and often to provide economic assistance as well. Most people want the best for their new grandchildren, so they sacrifice in whatever ways they can. In spite of what seems to be a liberalization of views, early sexual activity has about the same consequences it ever did, and the stakes are even higher now with the threat of AIDS.

If your family has an opportunity to view a sensitive film or video showing the realities of childbirth and the family's role in it, be sure to watch it together. Young men need to understand their role in pregnancy and childbirth. They need to learn that they too are vulnerable and that in marriage they can benefit from a woman's strength.

Certainly exposure to reality is better than the half-truths so commonly presented. Do our sons and daughters have the correct information? Are they aware of our values and those of our extended families in matters of sexual expression? If there is a vacuum in the home, young people will depend primarily on their peers and the media's manipulation for answers.

Alcohol and Other Concerns

Another issue parents need to address when discussing sexuality is alcohol. One of the most harmful effects of drinking is the removal of sexual restraints. Where there is little else to occupy the time or where peer pressure is strong, youth may well use and abuse alcohol. The combination of alcohol and youthful sexuality can produce tragic results: having sexual intercourse when neither partner had planned to, date rape, assaults, and other injurious sexual behaviors.

According to newspaper reports and surveys today, it is the unusual young person who is not sexually active. The words "lost virginity" have lost their original value orientation. Films and articles about sex describe the first sex experience as a loss of innocence that is almost like a burden.

Sexual activity should be determined by individuals according to their intent and feelings for each other within the guidelines from their church and their family. Parents can counteract the impression that "everybody is doing it" by helping their children realize that sexual activity is a private matter, not a matter for boasting. The ideal is to be married before one enters into the union of sexual intercourse. What has experience to do with it? The experience of learning to express love physically will be a lifelong activity, and we will never reach the end of its joy if, as partners, we are completely concerned for each other. The values of the church are clear on this point, so why should we try to avoid teaching them? If our children choose to do differently, they know what our principles are.

How can we prevent our children from receiving double messages regarding sexuality? If they grow up knowing that they will need to adjust to the discipline of marriage and expecting to make a life in it, they will not need to be influenced by outside messengers.

The AIDS crisis has produced startling clarity about the negative consequences of unwise sexual activity. Parents are still the primary ones to warn about the lack of "safe sex." Peers and media often give youth the impression that they may engage in sexual activity without responsibility. We need to help our growing children understand that sexual satisfaction is similar to many other pursuits in life. In spite of romantic notions of happy endings as long as both partners "want" sex, the congruence between sexual experience and emotional satisfaction will have to be learned and practiced. Those who do learn are blessed.

How Self-Esteem Influences Our Sexual Life

Self-esteem plays a vital role in our sexual life. Children who suffer depression may, when in their teens, continue to think of themselves as worthless. Those who feel worthless will not value themselves enough to protect themselves from sexual aggression or have the emotional strength to determine for themselves when they should be sexually active.

The courage to be in the world but not of it is especially difficult in a society that puts so much emphasis on sex. Advertisers exploit sexually attractive men and women by using their sexuality to sell a wide variety of products. Hair with a particularly unrestrained look, lips enticingly red, eyes outlined prominently, and hips shaped and draped tastefully may make a young teen wonder if she can ever become so attractive. According to what she sees, self-worth depends on outward appearance.

Self-esteem established throughout childhood helps protect children from sexual or other abuse. Children with good self-esteem are more likely to say no and will dare to speak up when compromising situations occur. Healthy self-esteem is a major factor in helping young people decide not to use power to dominate or oppress others or to give in to the unwelcome power and control of aggressive persons. Continual training in living as equals in society is the goal.

Specific problems such as weight or height can affect children's self-esteem. Eating disorders are common and are often associated with self-esteem. As parents we can look for medical help for some of the problems or see if our child is interested in meeting with a counselor or joining a support group.

Our children's confidence and self-esteem are strengthened as they see themselves as competent and able. We can help them gain confidence not only through family interaction and affirmation but also by encouraging and applauding their participation in family athletic or artistic activities that teach lifelong skills for living.

The church's message about our worth also strengthens us. The good news of God's great love that we hear in the Bible, in hymns, and from sermons in many ways says to us, "You are of great worth."

Three Problems Facing
Our Children Today

Three problems fairly new to us face our children.

The first is homosexuality. Homosexuality is not new, but our present concerns with it are. Behind our efforts today to secure civil rights for gay people is the growing awareness that few, if any, have chosen this orientation. Rather, they discovered that it was part of who they are. Now what to do? This is a very difficult question to answer wisely in our culture. The result has been an isolation of a gay community in which too often, since marriage seems to be denied them, sex purely for pleasure takes over. So those young people who recognize that they have the same-sex orientation need wise counsel. But because they often hide the fact of their orientation even from their parents, they are not likely to get it.

So what to do? First, face the possibility that one of your children may be gay. What will your attitude be? Will it be open enough for the son or daughter to tell you and feel accepted? In the past couple of years, we have had several of our friends who are parents come to us for help. Their adult son or daughter had just disclosed to them that they were gay. The parents were devastated. But to their credit, they have all overcome that initial reaction and now accept and love their gay children as they are—including the gay child's possible companion.

Once we know our children's orientation, we can encourage them against promiscuity. It is promiscuity and not homosexuality that is responsible for AIDS. Their relationship (if they have any) with their same-sex companion should be on the same monogamous and committed basis as we expect of heterosexual couples.

The second problem is that our children are maturing physically sooner. The onset of puberty in girls is as early as nine years of age. Pregnancies at eleven are not unknown. Boys are also maturing earlier, and we hear about males involved in sexual assaults at ever earlier ages. Yet emotional maturation and mental development have not accelerated at the same pace.

Our society is not training our youth for specific jobs and professions so that they can provide for a family at the time they become sexually mature. Students from other countries tell about their opportunity for vocational training, and yet they love our provisions for a broad education. Something in between would probably be the ideal, perhaps job training first and college afterwards if they choose. American students sometimes express concern that they may be locked into an educational direction that they may later wish to change. Providing job training first would be a protection in this regard. In frontier days young people entered into marriage fairly young and yet were able to support themselves. Perhaps someday someone will find a way to narrow the gap between sexual activity and financial responsibility.

The third problem is the longer time that children live at home. Our economy has been such that permanent homemaking is not always possible until young people are in their late twenties and early thirties. Fewer young people are connecting sexual activity with uniting with another in marriage to form a home.

The church needs to come to grips with these problems. As parents who have grounded ourselves in the Christian faith, we can certainly use our church's help here. Knowing where we stand and being clear about it is the best that we as parents can do. Our youth need to hear clear messages. We all should remember the struggles we went through to find our way. Looking to the church and the helpful resources that our communities have to offer will help us utilize the gospel to deal with these problems.

Our Sexuality with God as Parent

Our emphasis on success and large salaries obscures other values. Skills for forming friendships seem lacking. We fail to recognize the amount of time and effort it takes genuinely to know another person. We rarely see people being warned that sexual contact may be unfulfilling and that there are times when sexual relationships are not wanted—even in marriage. Our maturing children may know little about the difficulties married people experience as they sort out their sexual relationship. In a candid conversation a young woman said, "I wouldn't let my husband near me for three months after childbirth." Although this may sound extreme, it may be more common than expected.

Learning about sexuality under God with God as parent is a lifelong adventure. After many years of growing comes the reward: we begin to see the wonder and glory of sharing creation with God. God can use marriage and parenthood to reveal to us something about the divine nature.

▼

Things to Talk About and Do

1.   What positive memories do you have about affection between your parents and other couples you knew as a child?
2.   What role did your own self-esteem have in your sexual maturity and behavior? How can you enhance your children's self-esteem?
3.   What can you do to help your children in regard to the dark side of sex: sexual abuse, exploitation, rape, AIDS, and the media's distorted portrayals?

▼

Note

1.   Ellen Creager, "Keen Teen Role Model These Days? Probably Sexy R-Rated Films," *St. Paul Pioneer Press Dispatch*, 9 Mar., 1989, 8B.

7

Encouraging Creativity in Our Children

The meaning of Genesis 1:27, which says that God created male and female in the divine image, is that we are *creative*. The beginning of biblical instruction is that God created the heavens and the earth and all that is in them. We are made for creativity. We make choices. We are participating in the creation of our destiny.

In this chapter we will look at some ways to enhance creativity throughout childhood, beginning with infancy. Creativity is inborn and can be seen in the way babies interact with the environment. Exploration and discovery continue as children enter school and other adults encourage them. During preadolescent years, exercising creativity helps children build a foundation of self-esteem. Adolescents find themselves having to make choices about school subjects and activities; some feel that their creativity is thereby curtailed because choosing one activity (such as basketball) may mean that there will not be time for others they might enjoy (choir). However activities outside school, including those in church, can counter this problem.

Play Has a Serious Meaning

As we observe the play of children, we see their personalities through the choices they make. Naturalists have observed the young of many species of animals at play and conclude that while play appeals to us humans as entertainment, the purpose is serious. Through trial and error in a safe environment, the young animals are making sense of their surroundings. The patterns for survival are being learned and established. Our infants and children in many ways are doing the same thing. We learn through play to modify our environment.

What is creativity? The traditional definition is the ability to generate new forms and patterns from existing ones. Creativity produces an attitude of expectancy and trust because the person sees many options and choices. As our children learn to see creative possibilities as they play and investigate the world, they are more likely to live richer and more enjoyable lives.

▼

As our children learn to see creative possibilities as they play and investigate the world, they are more likely to live richer and more enjoyable lives.

Trust comes from God who will reveal new ways for us under divine guidance. To expect to be able to cope with life's challenges builds self-confidence. We respect the wisdom of the aged because it shows that these challenges have been met.

Trust begins with the beginning of life. Throughout the Bible the worth of children is stressed. Some aspects of the ancient world were not hospitable to children, and Jesus warned against hindering and destroying children's self-esteem and even said that "it is to such as those that the kingdom of heaven belongs" (Matt. 19:14). Each borning cry of an infant means new hope to the human race. Christmas has a significance far bigger than sentiment. A new source of creativity had entered the world. Jesus came as an infant and his saving love and gave us our worth as adopted children of God, and we now share in Jesus' heritage. God will express a new creation in every child.

The Heroic Esther

The biblical character of Esther combines creativity and heroic action. Her story represents a message of courage and purpose. "Who am I and why am I here?" is the question answered in the story of Esther. She was probably little more than a child when she became the powerful queen. In a reversal of power she became the ruler of her uncle Mordecai who had served as her guardian. Even though she had little power as a female child, Esther as queen had become the only hope of her people, the Hebrews. In essence, Mordecai warned her, "Do not think that because you are queen, you can escape your racial destiny." A terrible plot had been hatched to destroy the Jews. Mordecai was very clear and told her that she might be able to save her people and herself. "Who knows? Perhaps you have come to royal dignity for just such a time as this" (Esther 4:14). Esther considered her options and just as single-mindedly replied, "I will go to the king, though it is against the law; and if I perish, I perish" (4:16). The king decided who would live and be heard, and if he chose not to listen to her, she would perish. However, the king listened to Esther and saved her people from the plot. This story is an illustration of a heroic and creative person who can inspire courage and creativity in us all. The least of all citizens, a young woman, suddenly became powerful, saw her destiny, and fulfilled it.

Letting Babies and Preschoolers Have Freedom

One of the joys in having babies is watching their creativity. When we congratulated a father recently on his new baby, he said, "Oh, I could stay home all day to watch her grow!" What a privilege it is for those of us who can do just that! But when we need to be away at work part of the time, we may better appreciate the time we do have to observe a baby's rapid development and eagerness for life.

A baby reaches out to its siblings, if there are any, and to other children. Why does a baby know how to play with another baby? It does, and their interaction is very creative. The socialization process begins in those earliest months. Parents who are at ease with themselves will let their child react according to his or her preferences and discover a wonderful arena for watching growth. Unfortunately some parents are not comfortable enough to let a baby or young child exercise freedom. If this happens, it is good to know something is awry and seek help. A wish, unconscious or otherwise, to thwart the child is not healthy. A parent can recognize the need for help without falling into despair. A mark of maturity is to seek help. Trained helpers in child care can be good people to ask for referrals.

Babies and small children instinctively sense the opposite sex. This is not a matter for teasing but one to treat with respect. These little ones are exploring their environment and their identity as male and female. Parents of small children appreciate the visitor who treats their child with dignity when the child shows this sexual awareness.

Encouraging School-Age Creativity

At school age, children often remind a parent who is giving directions, "I have a teacher now." Parents now share direction giving. If the child has been in preschool or daycare, he or she already has made this adjustment.

In the grade-school years, the children's creative processes have developed so much that if provided materials, space, and a little encouragement, they can soar. Some build playhouses or redecorate their rooms. Some collect rocks, shells, insects, or stamps. Some develop music skills, others try writing, and many read a lot. Their creativity can also be encouraged by going to museums, touring a historical site, factory, or other interesting place, playing sports, and acting in plays.

The attraction of video games may prevent some children from developing creativity. Parents need to provide a wide variety of activities to minimize the amount of unstructured time used for video games.

When school begins, children live more scheduled lives. The times parents can enter into the child's creative ventures may be limited to weekends and vacations. Schoolwork and lessons fill the weekday routines, and we were glad to have it so. We hardly have the time and expertise to present enough learning and socialization experiences for our children.

We hear today of "quality time." The benefit of quality time has been the awareness that children need some special attention. The detriment is that parents feel guilty unless their time with their children is somehow outstanding or memorable. When does time with children get that label? Unless there is a seriously injurious effect on parent and child, time spent together is quality time. Our children often told their Grandma when they visited, "Grandma, you don't have to do anything; I just like to be here!"

Children who play alone feel very secure in their environment because they feel safe enough to ignore it. Children who invent games and ideas by themselves are being very creative. They are interacting with their own powers and finding resources within themselves to be satisfactory. They are finding a balance of being with parents, peers, and themselves and learning to be content, a pattern which will continue for a lifetime. This balance is another mark of our individuality. As the Myers-Briggs inventory (see Chapter 5) points out, all degrees of extrovert and introvert are gifts to society. It is all right to be ourselves.

The Importance of Preadolescent Creativity

Some educators overrate the diagnostic ability of tests. If we would give only *some* credence to intelligence tests, we would be serving children better. How was it that at your high-school reunion all of the successful people were not "A" students? We are born with gifts; bad circumstances can prevent us from fulfilling our promise. But stronger than other factors is the application of creative potential. So we can always be surprised at how life turns out!

Preadolescent creativity has a purpose. We wish we had known how important it is to build self-esteem in children at this stage. These are the teaching years, and skills and values can be taught. Because children at this time are so delightful, the dread of the approach of adolescence may prevent us from realizing the value of this stage. This is the time to get to know our children and form a good relationship as an investment for the future. The influence of scout leaders, church workers, and others who take an interest in children remain with them always.

During this time children are at the peak of their creativity. Unless culturally deterred, they like to learn about anything. They like to test their skills and enjoy working with peers. They tackle a task enthusiastically and will work for symbolic rewards like ribbons and badges. Children follow the general requirements of their projects but turn them into individualized products.

I (Lucy) would not have missed my years as a scout leader! The rewards of providing girls with the opportunity to be creative and to stretch their abilities are greater than anyone can imagine who has not done it. When adolescence comes and turns their world upside down, this esteem and skill are like money in the bank.

When they participate in planning, children of this age are the best examples in brainstorming—casting out of ideas without critical evaluation. Brainstorming is especially appropriate at this age because preadolescent children match their ideas with the ability to carry them out.

In workshops stressing the development of creativity, brainstorming is at the beginning. For any troubling situation the questions "What can I do?" and "What do I want to happen?" are most important. Children who make good use of brainstorming learn to see reality and to understand when circumstances cannot be changed. They know when fantasy is appropriate and when it is not.

Creativity in the High-School Years

One of Bill's students seemed to be able to do anything; he was not afraid to set up any program and easily took initiative. When asked how this happened, John reflected that he had gone to high school in a small town in South Dakota. There he had to play on the basketball team because there were just enough boys for a team; during the half time he played trombone because he was needed in the pep band; and at the end of the game he sold candy and popcorn because there were never enough students for that task.

His high-school experience was certainly different from our children's in a suburban school. When they went to high school, if they played an instrument well enough for the band or orchestra, that was their extracurricular activity. When one of our daughters wanted to be in debate but also wanted DECCA (an organization for business students), she really had to fight for it. Our other children faced similar dilemmas. Student participation in any extracurricular activity made demands on after-school and weekend time also. Coaches and teachers can be very cross with students who take any time from the activity they direct.

John's experience was the more productive one, allowing him to sample several fields without feeling that he had to stay in any of them. For some talented students, perhaps being able to concentrate on developing a particular gift is good. As a musician, our younger son comes into contact with many performers who have done just that. However, they wonder whether a broader approach might have served them better.

Long-time studies show that creativity can be taught. Leaders and educators are invited every year to spend a week at Buffalo State University at an annual Creative Problem Solving Institute sponsored by the Creative Education Foundation. Several large corporations also send representatives for training. Nationally known leaders in the field plan a week's activity to teach a step-by-step approach to creative problem solving. They begin with formal training and practice in brainstorming and finish by using many training methods to teach the participants how to find as many options as possible for solving a problem. Many teachers and social workers who work with children are present and many come yearly.

> ▼
>
> **If God is the Eternal Yes, do we say yes to our children?**

Some Practical Steps for Encouraging Creativity

How, then, can we enhance creativity in our children? Over the years as church workers, scout leaders, teachers, and parents, we have found some helpful guiding principles for enhancing a child's creativity.

Encourage Enthusiasm. Very little creativity happens without this ingredient. True enthusiasm for life and learning come from our attitude toward life. Naturally we are not always enthusiastic, but we can ask ourselves, "If God is the Eternal Yes, do we say yes to our children?" Search through your pleasant memories. Do they include many where someone was very enthused about you and something you were doing?

A young girl named Julie decided to choose gardening as her 4-H project even though she knew it would not be easy. Her parents encouraged her and gave her part of their garden plot as her own. She planted, hoed, and weeded all summer. When the time came for the county fair, Julie chose the best vegetables and flowers to exhibit. She and her family went to the fair after the prizes had been awarded and were delighted to see that Julie's flowers had won a red ribbon and her vegetables a blue ribbon. Her father in particular was delighted. Not only did he compliment Julie, but later he called his parents and others to tell them what a good job his daughter had done. This greatly built Julie's self-esteem and provided her with confidence for future projects.

I (Lucy) still remember a time when my father ridiculed a creative-writing project that our teacher constructed. I had received acclaim for my paper but my father did not think it worthwhile. It hurt. Parents should not feel they must give false praise, but we need to be aware of the long-term effects of squelching enthusiasm. Not every effort of our children's should be praised. Children soon learn to evaluate that praise as worthless, but honest enthusiasm builds confidence. "The reward of a job well done is the ability to do a harder one," says the old aphorism. Lack of enthusiasm cuts off the natural progression.

Be Creative Yourself. To be creative ourselves is perhaps the best motivator for our children to be creative. Do you enjoy making something? Often we do, but then we compare what we have done to what others have done, and that can be very discouraging. Children often face similar competition. The most devastating competition is within our own families. "She's the pretty one." "He's the only coordinated one in the family." Such stereotyping is not easy to overcome. Jealousy and defeat accompany such comparisons.

Many of us are still dealing with some of the emotions of jealousy and shame suffered earlier in life. Such feelings often keep us from trying new things. We fear failure. We attack ourselves as *being* failures and have labeled ourselves as inferior at an early age. Learning to deal with the disabling emotions of jealousy and lack of initiative is a real push toward adulthood. Eventually there is a balance between winning and losing, but to the loser that does not seem to matter. Eventually if a person has enough experience, jealousy is easier to handle, but it may never completely go away. Dealing with failures over the years is more important than dealing with success. As parents, our courage to attack new projects and to share emotions on an appropriate level provides healthy models for our children.

Limit TV. Limiting the amount of time our children watch television and play video games makes space for creativity. Perhaps the family can look through the guide from the newspaper together and plan what programs to watch and what times the TV will be shut off. Some of the programs are wonderful in educational and human-interest content. Families who watch them together and discuss the contents are spending quality time together. Visual images do stimulate our minds and stay with us.

▼

Learning to deal with the disabling emotions of jealousy and lack of initiative is a real push toward adulthood.

Once we removed some of the parts from our TV to keep our daughter from watching it continuously. Even though that was a traumatic time for her, she later realized she needed the intervention. Our children have thanked us for not using the TV as a baby-sitter. They learned to be self-directed and in college were able to enjoy academic pursuits while too many of their fellow students were still addicted to TV. Getting an education demands more concentration and patience than many people ever develop.

Tell Stories Together. Making our own images by reading or listening helps us rely upon our own imagination as well. Telling stories of our family is another way to spark the imagination. Our children identify even more with the characters in the family stories than with fictional ones. One story from my (Lucy's) family about in-law trouble was told to us by my mother about my father's grandfather, who did not like the man his daughter intended to marry. A man wanting to exploit the situation asked Grandpa, "Whatcha going to do when Sarie marries Will?" Grandpa replied, "I'll just put another plate on the table." I have passed this story on to my children. Inventing stories and story telling are creative skills.

Provide a Place for Creativity. An environment for creating may not be easy to find or arrange. We consider ourselves consumers instead of creators. "Where did you buy that?" Instead of being factories where our needs for food and clothing are met, our homes meet the need of taste arbiters in magazines, newspapers, and TV. Few of us probably remember the fruit cellars where food was stockpiled by the family's efforts. That room was remodeled in the 1940s to become a rec-room or a den and eventually became a family room primarily for watching TV. Today the family room has virtually become a second living room that must be decorated by current taste to compete with others in the neighborhood. Hardly anywhere does a child have space to put up a project that requires time and decision making. Today's homes are often too neat for experimenting. Let your children use the kitchen or part of the garage or a corner of some other room for their creative pursuits.

Helping children keep things somewhat organized can be creative. Having plastic dishpans or baskets for the children's materials keeps at least some of the supplies in one place. Agreeing on a time for throwing out projects that no longer hold anyone's interest is a good idea, otherwise your home may seem booby-trapped with half-completed projects.

Keep "Found" Material. Having supplies at hand is an incentive for children to be creative. If they have to ask for each item they need and go to the store several times, the urge to try something may soon be lost. However, cans, bottles, fabric scraps, or other found materials provide a good beginning.

At a workshop on creativity, a small group received a cardboard core from a roll of wrapping paper. Everyone around the circle pantomimed a use for the core. No one could repeat any suggestions from before. The whole idea was to stir up new ways of seeing the core. Some ideas included using it as a musical instrument, a mailing tube, a pencil holder, and a flower vase. We had our minds challenged.

One of our sons did a project of this type on his own. When he found discarded plastic items around the house, he saved them and fastened them together to make a large spaceship. Painted with aluminum paint, it actually looked like one. A neighbor, noticing him playing with the ship, said enthusiastically, "You should enter that in the state fair." With her recommendation he did, and he was further rewarded with a blue ribbon.

Play Together. Charades and dramas are fun for the whole family. Some of our best times as a family have been playing charades and other games with other families. When we get together now, the children can recall who was the most creative in each game. Also enjoyable are board games like Monopoly and yard games like volleyball or touch football. When children become parents themselves, they want their children to enjoy similar good times.

Allow Time to Dream. All children need and deserve time to dream. One of the trends that we find hard to combat is our fear of boredom for children. Although there are laws against child labor and time to play or otherwise enjoy life is not a premium for our children, we still feel obliged to see that every minute of their time is occupied.

Many a good idea has sprung from unstructured time, from a mind engaged in dreaming. Children need to be allowed to know themselves and find out what their preferences really are. They need to have time to make their own choices as often as possible and find what they like. They need time to dream. Being bored is good sometimes because it can lead to independence from outside distractions and to a natural swing to activity of one's own choice. I (Lucy) hope we never go to year-round schools. Most children are ready for routine again after their hiatus from school in the summer.

Encourage Flexible Thinking and Acting. Flexible thinking and acting modeled by adults help children feel confident about their world: they see that there is more than one way to do things. A child may even be the one to offer another way. We spoke of the competition and jealousy that comes with comparison; now what can one do when something fails? Someone wins every competition and someone loses. Teaching how to win and lose graciously is part of nurturing a child. Right from the beginning children need to learn that no one receives the same treatment as others from parents or anyone else. A sense of fairness means an awareness that my needs are recognized too. But this may not mean that I receive the same as others. Fairness also takes into consideration a person's individuality. While this is a difficult concept to understand, it leads to a mature acceptance of setbacks. Failure spurs us on to further creativity, to consider our options. If not this, what now? Speaking in honest praise about another way of handling the same problem helps our children to know that if one cannot do as one would like, there are other good ways and projects. One can be flexible and "make do" with one's situation.

▼

We and our children were created by God to be creative.

A teacher-training educator from New Guinea wrote, "This week the students are giving presentations on improvised teaching aids they have made and researched, using bush materials, junk and a big chunk of their own imagination and ingenuity. Look at those paintings made with flower petals and tree roots and see those nifty paint brushes made from betal nut shell husks. Heri Lom is holding a ball he made from banana leaves; it is perfectly round; works great for physical education skills. Aba models a doll made out of runaigrass, others made puppets and many other things . . . these young teachers are going to be thankful for essential books and will be quite able to make many of their own teaching aids."

We call this superior education!

Delight In But Do Not Take Over. One factor that can greatly dampen children's creativity is the tendency for adults to take over their children's projects. When we are tempted (and aren't we all!) to take over, we need to exercise strong restraint. With our own and other children, we have observed that our overinvolvement works detrimentally to a child's confidence in his or her ability to do a project. When we invest too much of ourselves in our child's project because we are aware of his or her talents, showing this even by the use of praise, the child may begin to feel it is no longer his or her project and may well mess it up. Have we not felt this pressure when we were overly praised for our talents and did more poorly as a result?

When a project leaves our home and goes to a school or fair, we want it to show that we as a family are capable people. Science projects and book reports often reveal a parent's effort with a child's signature. We not only noticed the project, we took it over. Other siblings can get involved as well. "What I can do when no matter what our youngest child does, the older one takes it from him to finish?" This is even harder than restraining a parent! Drawing that line between encouragement and wanting to work on the project ourselves is very difficult. Almost all parents have a really hard time here. Let the project belong to the one who thought of it and is doing it. Sharing a project is fun and if it is appropriate, very fine. But most college papers should not be signed, "Mom and me!"

In the Image of God

We and our children were created by God to be creative. But, as this chapter has shown, sometimes we need help in knowing how to encourage our children's creative development. However, even if we make mistakes and look back in dismay, knowing we could have done better, our children are resilient. They may be creative in spite of us, not just because of us.

We can relax in the wisdom, love, power, and forgiveness of God, enjoying the good times and letting God heal those times that didn't go well.

▼

Things to Talk About and Do

1.   Think of a time in your life when someone encouraged your creativity and applauded your efforts. Do you remember a time when your creativity was squelched?

2.   Recall a situation in which you felt your children's choices were too risky or dangerous. What did you do? Have you ever felt that you needed to push your children a little toward *more* risky choices because they wanted to "play it safe"?

3.   Look over the following list and think of the ways you have already done many of these things. Then read the list again, choose a couple of items that you want to work on, and write down some new things you plan to do.

Encourage enthusiasm
Be creative yourself
Limit TV
Tell stories together
Provide a place for creativity
Provide a variety of materials
Play together
Allow time to dream
Encourage flexible thinking and acting
Delight in but do not touch

▼▼▼

8

Blessing Our Children

▲▲▲

An editorial writer, reflecting on tragic events in which human life was destroyed, said, "It is beyond comprehension, such cruel waste. But it can bring forth one good . . . . It can renew a resolve to say the kindly word that crosses the mind, to follow the generous impulse, to make good the good intention, to scribble the admiring note or the sympathetic letter, to speak at every parting the quiet tidings of affection and encouragement."[1]

A rather unusual observation for a newspaper editorial. But how true! And how directly applicable to our parenting. What the editorial advocates is what Scripture calls "giving a blessing."

Blessing in the Bible

In his book *The Wounded Parent,*[2] Guy Greenfield discusses the marvelous opportunity parents have to bless their children. He refers to the Old Testament custom of fathers blessing their children, as illustrated in the story of Jacob and Esau.

Although they were twins, Esau was considered the oldest because he emerged first from Rebecca's womb. Esau was his father Isaac's favorite while Jacob was his mother's favorite. When Isaac was old and blind, he asked Esau to hunt his favorite game, prepare the food, and then come to him for his blessing. Rebecca wanted Jacob to have the oldest son's blessing, so she prepared a meal of lamb for Jacob to give to Isaac. She also put the lamb's skins on Jacob's hands so that he would feel as hairy as Esau to his father. Jacob then asked for the blessing. As Isaac felt Jacob, Isaac said, "The voice is Jacob's voice, but the hands are the hands of Esau . . . . Are you really my son Esau?" He answered, "I am" (Gen. 27:22-24), and he received his brother's blessing. When Esau returned, the ruse was discovered, and Jacob had to flee for his life. But once the blessing was given, it could not be taken back.

▼

Blessing our children helps them to feel good about themselves, to develop their interdependence, self-esteem, and self-reliance.

In the New Testament the practice of blessing is universalized. St. Peter writes, "Do not repay evil from evil or abuse for abuse, but, on the contrary, repay with a blessing for to this you were called—that you might inherit a blessing" (1 Pet. 3:9). The root of the Greek word here for "bless" is *eulogeo,* which means "to speak good to someone." Blessing our children goes beyond speaking, of course, but it includes and perhaps even centers on speaking.

The well-known story in the New Testament about blessing is happier than the one just recounted from the Hebrew Scripture. Parents were bringing their small children to Jesus that he might touch them. Jesus' disciples saw this as a nuisance and rebuked the parents. But Jesus silenced them and said, "'Let the little children come to me; do not stop them; for it is to such as these that the kingdom of God belongs . . . .' And he took them up in his arms, laid his hands on them and blessed them" (Mark 10:14,16).

Jesus gave his blessing by touching people (see Chapter 6). After touching them, laying his hands on them, holding them in his arms, Jesus *blessed* them. We know from the Old Testament what blessing them meant—to say good words about them to them and to invoke God's favor on them.

In his letter to the Romans, St. Paul writes, "Each of us must please our neighbor for the good purpose of building up the neighbor" (15:2). The word translated here as "building up" is *oikodomay,* which is translated in other versions as "edify." We derive the English word "edifice," meaning an imposing building, from that Greek word. To edify or build up means to facilitate another's growth—in short, to bless.

Words That Bless

What we do for our neighbor we do for our children, because they are our closest neighbors. We bless them by saying good words about them to them, by reinforcing them, by supporting them in their own creativity, and by affirming their own identity. This prepares them to move out and beyond us—to leave father and mother. Blessing them helps them to feel good about themselves, to develop their interdependence, self-esteem, and self-reliance. As children are blessed, they internalize the blessing, making it their own.

Each child has his or her own "place" in this world. Each child has his or her own unique value. If we label our children as good boy, bad boy, graceful girl, or clumsy girl, we put a straitjacket on the development of their own uniqueness. Labeling prevents or substitutes for creative thinking. The same can be said for comparisons. How can one compare uniqueness?

Psychotherapist Lawrence LeShan applies this uniqueness of each individual to the way a physician should treat a patient. An "axiom of holistic medicine," he writes, "is that each person is unique and each program must be individualized." As an illustration he quotes Rabbi Nachmann of Bratislava: "God calls one man with a shout, one with a song, and one with a whisper."[3]

In like manner we parents are challenged to know our children in their uniqueness so that we know whether a shout, a song, or a whisper can best help them develop their own unique person, their own distinct creativity. Rebecca wanted her son Jacob to have Esau's blessing, not his own. So it is tempting to wish one child were more like another, or like a neighbor child. This is the parent's problem, not the child's. The solution is to discover the uniqueness of the child by removing all comparison labels so that the child has a chance to make himself or herself known to us.

The Unblessed

Larry came for counseling because he was a frustrated parent. In spite of the fact that he had been determined to do things differently from his own parents, he found himself doing the same things. And his children, he believed, were feeling the same way he did as a child. The counselor encouraged him to relive his childhood. Larry came from a home in which both parents believed that criticism was the way to shape up a child. Because his father left the bulk of the parenting to the mother, hers was the image that came most clearly to Larry's mind. A demanding person, "she was good at letting me know where I was lacking," he said wryly. "Nothing I did was ever good enough—or if it was, she kept this to herself." This critical pressure sent Larry into an endless quest for perfection to avoid his mother's criticism, but even more, to gain her approval. It was a fruitless quest. His parents had not received from their own families what Larry wanted from them. Both seemed unable to break out of this conditioning, no matter how hard Larry tried to please them. Even if they were pleased, even if they had positive feelings toward Larry, they couldn't express them. How sad!

When we feel we are not good enough, no one else seems good enough either. Such a critical attitude is continually at work in the way we look at others, so that we enjoy so little and receive even less. Instead of being thankful for what we have, we discount it. This attitude toward life undermines the health of body, mind, and spirit and is destructive to our relationships.

In parenting, many of us try to live up to the expectations of others. What is a "good" parent? For most of us a good parent is one whose children are "doing well." But if this is true, being a good parent is a very tenuous position, contingent upon things beyond our control. Guy Greenfield puts this well. "We [parents] tend to feel good about ourselves when our children seem to be doing well and down on ourselves when they are not. In neither case are we aware of the grace that is at work, or that our own role as a believer may be as important as what we do or don't do in parenting."[4]

Unblessed parents like Larry pass on their *unblessing* to their children, unless they realize their predicament and seek help. Larry needs to be blessed in order to bless. Through his counselor who serves as a temporary parent figure, Larry can receive God's blessing. He can follow a new route to inner peace with himself through a love that has no conditions attached to it. His children will notice the difference. The serenity of believers who know they are blessed is contagious. The self-esteem of those who are at home with grace is persuasive.

Each generation seriously needs to take the meaning of being blessed to the next generation because we tend to pass on, verbally or nonverbally, what we have received. This responsibility for the next generation, however, is too much for any individual family. It takes more than parents. We need the extended family as well to bless our children. The isolation of the family as a unit in itself is not a biblical model. The biological bonding of the extended family is often not possible in our urbanized society, but those strong family bonds still exist in many third-world countries. Perhaps this is no great loss because we still have the spiritual bonding of a different extended family in the fellowship of believers. The church in its local congregations can be the extended family we need for the blessing of our children.

▼

The serenity of believers who know they are blessed is contagious. The self-esteem of those who are at home with grace is persuasive.

Seeing Our Congregation as an Extended Family

The local congregation is a family-like community called into existence by the gospel of God's forgiving love. The gathering of this community to hear this good news over and over again helps to clear communication problems in our families. Reassured of God's forgiveness and acceptance, members of the community are encouraged to forgive themselves and others. The community gathers to worship together this God of forgiving love. Nearly all congregations include in their worship service a confession of sins, followed by an assurance of divine forgiveness.

The congregation is also a community that calls each person and the family. Through the gospel we are called to a life of meaning and purpose under God. This calling is fitted to the uniqueness of the person.

Being parents is an expression of our calling, and we can feel good about this calling. We too need reinforcement and support so that we can release our best in this endeavor. Even when we feel discouraged about our parenting, perhaps we are doing as best we can considering our hangups and bondage to past conditioning. We need help and not judgment, hope and not guilt. With help we can be liberated from our past conditioning.

Classes and support groups for parents can be very helpful toward this end with both the guidance of the teacher or leader and the sharing and support of other parents of the class. For example, we have conducted a series called "A Biblical Approach to Parenting" for Sunday morning adult forums in congregations. And most pastors are willing to counsel parents who feel the need for more personal help.

The congregation is a community that encourages trust in a Power beyond our own—in the God who created, redeems, and empowers us. This encouragement can reduce the pressure we feel when it seems we are all alone in our parenting. Reminders of this trust can be found in our worship services where the purpose of the prayers, hymns, Scripture readings, and sermon is to remind, to relive, to reinforce our faith. If your experience is like ours, it may take effort to keep your mind on the service, to become involved as a participant. Repeated words and music have a way of losing our attention, but this very repetition has the potential for giving us the spiritual renewal that we need. They remind us of God's deliverance in the past so we will trust God for the future. They remind us of answered prayer so that we feel encouraged to pray—for guidance in our parenting, for our children, for our marriage, for the extended family of the congregation. We can pray also for ourselves, for whatever changes in attitude we need in order to be open to receiving the help for which we ask. Finally each worship service includes the corporate expression of praise—thankfulness to God for all that God has given us. This helps us to focus on what we have in order to grow in appreciation of these blessings.

The local congregation is a prophetic as well as a supportive community. It has a mission to society. A community within the larger community, the congregation serves as a watchdog, monitoring how people treat one another. The congregation shares the passion of Christ for justice and respect and is sensitive to oppression and exploitation. Children are often the victims of societal exploitation. As this community of faith within the larger community joins with other congregations, it can often exert the needed influence on the power structures of this larger community to effect desired changes. Those in positions of power in our society are seen by the congregation as expressing their calling in this function. They are serving as authorities under God.

The Church's Nurturing Presence

We often do not give much thought to talking to others about our faith, but our attendance, support, and fellowship tell those around us that God is important in our lives. Our contributions provide the means for programs and classes for parents and show our resolve to be of nurturing help.

When I (Lucy) taught high school in a rural community after World War II, I felt the lack of a church as never before. It was the only time that I ever lived in a community without a church. The students had no spiritual community. In the classrooms there was no spirit of good will. One group continually belittled another. During the war, people from another state moved in to work in a nearby defense plant. The original residents were determined to keep them from belonging to the community. Each day brought a struggle between the two groups. Epithets and blows were readily traded. The youth of both groups had forgotten civil values; sexual immorality or talk of it abounded. The adults ignored the situation.

Together another teacher, my landlady, and I explored the possibility of opening an abandoned church. A retired Methodist minister agreed to come and hold services regularly. He went to the men's gathering place, the pool hall, and spoke to the male leaders in the community. They came to the church when it opened. There was a dramatic change in that town. A young couple in the community started a youth program in the church. They had wanted to do so for a long time. Children were drawn to the church and adults began to be concerned again. Today, that community has a new church building and a proud congregation.

Teachers belonging to congregations are a help in combining the functions of the school and church. In our pluralistic society some schools seem to have lost their function of teaching values. The teachers know from their experience that the church needs to fill some of those gaps for children.

A school wishing to establish a reputation for scholastic or athletic superiority often leaves very little room for the average performer in these fields. The church can be of help here. In a church-connected scout troop, I (Lucy) found that giving praise and acceptance to children who were not otherwise recognized was something scouting could do.

Another example of ways a congregation can help comes from a church youth leader. A long feud between children from a poor rural area and those in town was stopped when the church youth leader demanded that open showers be fitted with doors for privacy because his group was taunted for their poor clothing. Some children's poor social behavior is shame-based for similar obvious reasons. The church is blessing its children when it takes seriously their pain.

Perhaps the larger benefit to the child comes from the church that makes the parents feel at ease and accepted. Many young parents feel depressed and defeated by parenting. Many parents are struggling with specific problems with their children, such as underachievement, dyslexia, attention-deficit syndrome, or mental or physical illness or handicaps. In their church home, the message of hope and acceptance is given as a gift to them. As the parents grow, they are empowered to help others as only those who have faced those problems can help, and they become a great resource to other parents.

The Church Nurtures Its Specific Community

Not many years ago a home burned down in our church neighborhood. Relief in specific forms was gathered quickly to give the family a home again. They contributed bedding, clothes of the right size, and household goods. Many other needs were also filled. Although this family attended our church, they were not members. But the local congregation felt that this family was theirs. We can be sure that this act of charity made an impression upon the children from this disrupted family and eased their trauma.

Many churches reach out to the local community as they see a need. Stay-at-home moms are a group that has gained attention again in our church community. The needs of these mothers and children are often forgotten. The mothers seldom get a break from child care. They long for intellectual stimulation so that they can be more fulfilled. So the neighborhood mothers meet regularly at the church for discussion and support.

Another need for parents that churches can meet is to provide young parents with opportunities to learn what the norms are for their developing children. When this group of parents comes together at the church for parental enrichment, the emphasis is on playing with the child in such a way as to develop maturity in speech and muscular coordination. Today the diagnostic ability of early childhood specialists can prevent many later disabilities. The key for such stimulation to enhance development is often the mother or father. The needed skills can be learned. Some churches see this kind of ministry as "their" program.

▼

As the parents grow, they are empowered to help others as only those who have faced those problems can help.

Some churches have opened daycare centers, a blessing to working parents. Safe daycare is not always available. To have daycare near the home is a great help for many children and their parents. Often churches have space and equipment that has long been unused or only used on Sunday.

One church which had a connecting nursing home installed a daycare center where senior citizens logged many volunteer hours. The director kept statistics proving that there were fewer physician visits made to the home after the daycare facility opened. Another church provided parents with a directory of persons capable of sick-child care in their homes. The parents made their own arrangements from the list.

Opportunity for Using Experience

The saying "Train up a child in the way he or she should go and walk there yourself once in awhile" is not only humorous but true. If children can see adults modeling to the best of their ability, they will gain more from those examples than from any theory. Comparing the church to a human body, St. Paul says, "If one member suffers, all suffer together with it" (1 Cor. 12:26). When a child suffers, he or she will be helped by the modeling of an adult who shows that one can start over after a failure. So much rides on success and accomplishment today that children wonder if they can ever "make it." Their fear of failure can keep them from trying. An adult model who accepted failure and started over may impress a child more than one who has never experienced failure.

We often say after a trauma, "Life goes on!" Those for whom "life must go on" know the struggle and the self-discipline. Children grieve in these traumas, and if we have known shattering experiences, we can understand and be a blessing to them and others. Some larger churches have a special counselor for children in grief. They have found it to be a good investment.

The Church's Unique Role

The church has a vital lesson for the family: forgiveness. How else can any community keep functioning? Through learning and change we develop. That development cannot occur if we must always live with our past mistakes being drummed into our consciousness. Old stereotypes, even in parenting, must be given up as we learn ways of acceptance. One of the most effective strategies in any situation is to make a radical change in procedure. We can do this if we can leave the past in peace. Where but in the church is the concept so well understood? If we believe in the forgiveness of sins, we have the vision to remove the guilt and power of past mistakes and strike out in new ways. The church can do better here than the secular community.

Asking for God's help in blessing our children opens us up to receive because we know what we need. In this asking we can see ourselves as hopeful and not as hopeless or despairing. Parenting calls us to our creative talents, and if we present our needs to God in prayer, we receive the Spirit to lighten our touch. With our security in God, we need not take all the responsibility but only share it. Nowhere is it more difficult or more necessary to put trust into action than in being a parent. Nothing is better for a child than a parent who is what he or she is—a flawed, trusting-in-God parent with joy and not despair in his or her heart. Such a parent is a child's blessing.

▼

Things to Talk About and Do

1. How were you blessed as a child? Recall times when someone (parent, grandparent, others) spoke well of you or was kind to you.
2. What could you do or are you doing that lets your children know that you care about them and have confidence in them?
3. Do you have extended family members living nearby (your children's aunts, uncles, cousins, grandparents, others)? If few or none, who serves as an extended family to your children? What role does your congregation play as extended family?
4. What is your congregation doing or what could it do to be a blessing to families in your area?

▼

Notes

1. *St. Paul Pioneer Press,* 21 June, 1990, 10A.
2. Guy Greenfield, *The Wounded Parent* (Grand Rapids, Mich.: Baker Book House, 1982).
3. Lawrence LeShan, *Cancer as a Turning Point* (New York: Plume–Penguine, 1990), 127-28.
4. Greenfield, *The Wounded Parent,* 126.

▼▼▼

9

It Never Ends

▲▲▲

Once we are parents, we are parents for life. A friend whose children were all past the age of twenty-one but who continued to have needs and problems involving their parents, said in rather amazed enlightenment, "It never ends!"

No, it doesn't. But that's OK. Why should it end? The relationships change and parents of adult children have a different function from parents of younger children. Though we are friends, it is a unique friendship because we are still the parents. The dependence of childhood changes to the interdependence of adulthood. Our adult children may still need us for parental support, and we may need them for family support.

Accepting Joy and Pain

Once we are parents, our identity includes our children. They become part of our lives—we are a family system. What affects one affects all the others in the system. In a negative sense, this is the basis of unhealthy codependence, as when alcoholism is present in the family. The organization Adult Children of Alcoholics has been a great help for the children in families who have become codependent because of a parent's disease.

We are affected in our family systems by the joys of the others as well as the pains, but the pains seem to fix our attention more. Love involves us in pain. There is no detachment in love. People who love each other are bound together by compassion. They feel the other's pains as if they were their own, even though they are not. Compassion is a noble passion and though needing some balance and control, it should never be turned off because it is painful. Christ's suffering on the cross is an example of the compassion of God for God's people that forever binds us together.

When you choose to love, be prepared to suffer. Your parents took this risk when they gave birth to you or adopted you. You took this risk when you chose to marry. A risk can go either way. This is why wedding vows usually include "for richer, for poorer," and "in sickness and in health." As a single parent, your marriage may have had more negative aspects than the marriage could endure. On the other hand, as a part of a couple, you may feel that your marriage reaped the positive side of this risk.

You also took a risk when you became a parent. Your child could have been, or perhaps was, born with some kind of problem. You may have had enormous problems with the birth and early survival of your child. Or the whole event may have come with surprising ease. The problems also may not have developed until later years. One never knows.

The other side of the risk also is tantalizing. The joys of marriage and family can be as ecstatic as any experience on this earth. One can feel that one will burst with joy on numerous occasions. We have felt this; you may have also.

As we have stressed throughout this book, our own childhood plays a key role in the raising of our children. Because there are no perfect parents and no perfect homes, none of us had a perfect childhood. Some unresolved conflicts, unhealed wounds, self-rejecting memories, and images of shame may still linger on in our conscious or unconscious mind. It is good to reflect on these, regardless of what stage of parenting you are in, even to talk them over with a counselor, so that you don't subconsciously project these unresolved memories onto your children. We can all come to peace with our childhood, allowing the forgiveness of God to enable us to forgive ourselves, to forgive the child of our memories, and to forgive our parents. We should get whatever help we need to come to peace with our childhood memories, because this is perhaps the best legacy we can give our children.

Dealing with Disappointment

Despite our best intentions and preparation, there may well be times when we experience the bitter pain of disappointment in our parenting. Not all influences on our children come from us. We are not God. We cannot control everything—as much as we wish we could.

Gloria's experience is a good example of such unanticipated disappointment. While she had occasionally been disturbed by her husband's absorption in his work, which left her with more than her share of the parenting, she knew he loved his family dearly, and things seemed to be going well with the children.

Then came that awful day when the high school principal called and asked if Gloria could come to her office. Gloria's son Tim was there. He had been caught in a drug bust at the school. The police were also involved. Gloria's husband was out of town on one of his frequent business trips. She endured a painful and humiliating session in the principal's office and learned that Tim would have to make a juvenile court appearance in the near future.

Gloria's world was shattered. This wasn't supposed to happen to good Christian families. She was both frightened and angry—frightened about what this was going to mean to her and her family's future, and angry with Tim for "doing this to her" and with her husband for what she believed was his neglect.

She was also angry with her church because for some time she had known that the youth program was not giving Tim the support and sense of belonging that he needed from them. For a while she stayed away from church. When she returned, she went late and left early to avoid talking to anyone. People must know about it, she thought, because the families of some of Tim's friends were members of the church.

As she sank deeper into her depression, she had one thing going for her. She had a good relationship with her pastor. After a particularly bad night with little sleep, she swallowed her pride and called him for an appointment. The pastor was a careful listener, and she was able to pour out her feelings on the first visit. In subsequent appointments, the pastor helped her to see that God was not "out of it" as Gloria had feared. Rather, God could use the whole unhappy situation for Tim's growth,

Gloria's and her husband's growth, the growth of their marriage (which she realized now had been losing its spontaneity and joy), and growth in her mothering of Tim.

But Gloria herself needed to see everything in this light before she could be open to the good that could happen. After several more weeks of misery, she could. Today, though the family still regrets the incident, they are also thankful to God because of the way God had been using it for the family's welfare.

Our disappointments may not always turn out as well as they did for Gloria and her family. Sometimes, as we have noted, we may think that the dreams we have for our children have been irrevocably shattered. What then? The challenge then is to grieve our losses and to adjust to a reality that we do not like.

Grieving Our Losses

Parenting includes times of loss. The stages of a child's development, for example, can progress more rapidly than we anticipate. All of a sudden, our little girl is a young woman, and our little boy is taller than we are. While we are going through these stages, we may not appreciate them as much as we do in retrospect. We grieve over the end of the various chapters in our children's lives, as when we take the crib apart and store it in the attic, or realize that our children are too old for the toys that catch our attention in the stores. Finally the youngest child grows up, and we find it hard to "let go of the baby." Endings can be painful. They remind us of the final ending, death, and the reality of our mortality and the old age that usually precedes it.

The loss we experience may be more drastic than the end of stages of childrearing. It may be the actual death of a child. This, as we have mentioned, happened to us. People never anticipate standing at the grave of their child, but there we stood. Sally was a young adult when she died. She was married, pregnant, and living far from us. The death was sudden and tragic, and we were devastated for years afterward. But with God's healing power and with the help of supportive friends, we not only survived but became totally involved in life again. Yet Sally's birthdays and the anniversaries of her death still bring back the sadness of the loss.

Many who have faced such deep grief have found help from pastors, members of their congregations, counselors, friends, support groups, and audio and printed resources. Books such as Granger Westberg's *Good Grief* (Minneapolis: Fortress Press, 1971), Glen Davidson's *Understanding Mourning* (Minneapolis: Augsburg, 1984), and Edgar Jackson's *When Someone Dies* (Philadelphia: Fortress Press 1971) speak clearly to the needs of those who grieve.

▼

Parenting is a continuous tension between belonging and separating. Our children need to separate themselves from us, and do so again and again.

Parenting is a continuous tension between belonging and separating. Our children need to separate themselves from us, and do so again and again. At the same time, the separation doesn't end belonging. Our ties are forever. The family system may change with time but it does not end. Here is where Nouwen's analogy of host and guest to parent and child mentioned in Chapter 1 breaks down. The guest leaves and there may be no further development of the relationship. When the child leaves, the relationship changes but continues to develop and grow. Even our Sally is still in a sense a part of our family system.

When We Feel Disheartened

There may be times when we seem to be getting no satisfaction out of our parenting. You may be in one of these periods now, and at least know what they are like from past experience. These "down" times often come when our children are teenagers—a potentially difficult stage for both children and parents. You may wish you could send at least one of them out somewhere. Or maybe you yourself would like to leave and say with the psalmist, "O that I had wings like a dove! I would fly away and be at rest" (Ps. 55:6).

These are times when we do not receive what we had anticipated from our parenting. Sometimes we become too attached to our dreams and find it difficult to identify any satisfaction apart from the way we had envisaged it.

When Job in his sufferings complained that God was silent in the face of his pleas for help and answering none of his words, his counselor, Elihu, confronted him with the possibility that it was Job who was not hearing rather than God who was not speaking. "For God," he said, "speaks in one way, and in two, though people do not perceive it" (Job 33:12-14).

We received much from our children as they were growing up, but also not as we had anticipated. Our almost-grown children became involved in some justice issues and saw the need for major changes in our culture. Through our children, we became more sensitive to injustice in the world and to the suffering they were trying to stop. This awareness that we gained from our children's perspective has changed the way we pray and the way we give financially.

If you are feeling disheartened at this moment, don't give up! Things can change and they can change for the better. God is still present and God is still demonstrating love and wisdom. "Wait for the Lord" (Ps. 27:14). Let the words of St. Paul inspire you: "Let us not grow weary in well doing [our parenting is well doing], for in due season we shall reap, if we do not lose heart" (Gal. 6:9 RSV).

Recently we baby-sat our three-year-old grandson Alberto while our daughter was away on a business trip. When his mother phoned to see how things were, he asked to speak with her. "I love you, Mommy," he said. What joy those words must have brought to our daughter! At least we know what joy they brought to Grandma and Grandpa.

The Power That Sustains Us: God's Love

The power that sustains us in the joys and pains of raising children is the love that Alberto expressed. He didn't say, "I love you *because*" or "I love you *if*." He just said, "I love you." This is unconditional agape love that comes from our Heavenly Parent and sustains our families. It enables us to be honest in our approval or disapproval of our children's behavior because we are not accepting the child or rejecting the child on the basis of such approval or disapproval.

We love the *person* of our loved one, and know that God does too. We are open—vocal—in our acceptance of this person, we can be warm in our affection to this person's body, even when we are unhappy about his or her behavior. Children as well as adults need the continued reassurance of our love through bodily touch and affection—the sacramental communication of something that is spiritual but needs tangible expression.

Nothing can separate us—really—from our children, because nothing can separate us from our Heavenly Parent's love. St. Paul's glowing words say it so forcefully: "For I am convinced that neither death, nor life, nor angels, nor rulers, nor things present, nor things to come, nor powers, nor height, nor depth, nor anything else in all creation, will be able to separate us from the love of God in Christ Jesus our Lord" (Rom. 3:38-39). As we reflect on God's love and allow ourselves to receive it unconditionally, by grace, as a gift, we will be enabled to give it in some measure to our children.

Paradoxically, it is precisely this unconditional love, this acceptance of the person as he or she is, that is the greatest power for positive change in behavior. This is because it provides the inner security that children need to bring our their best. Yet it seems that we find this hard to believe. Since time began we have resorted to "the law" to bring about change. We depended on our criticism and judgment to do the job, but it backfired, because criticism and judgment by themselves—particularly when we get a steady dose—disturb our inner security and lower our self-image. The result is that our confidence decreases and our worst is brought out. And yet some continue to persist in this counterproductive approach. Helping others feel good about themselves is a basic principle of conflict management, and it applies to family conflict as well. What makes us feel good about ourselves? Knowing we are loved and hearing it again and again with lots of hugs and affection.

Life Is Both Joys and Sorrows

Both joys and sorrows go with life in this world. As Christians, we refer to them symbolically as crucifixions and resurrections. There could be no resurrection of Christ—no Easter—unless there had been a crucifixion—a Good Friday. Joy and pain are interrelated. How much pain and how much joy do we have as parents? This may be a difficult question to answer, partly because some of us have a hard time tolerating pain and perhaps even subconsciously block it out. So we tend to deny the problems that should be obvious. Others of us have difficulty with joy. Perhaps we have become so used to being without joy that we don't recognize the opportunities for receiving it. Also, many of us have remembered our pains longer than we remember our joys. The negatives seem to stick with us longer and occupy more of our attention than the positives.

So all of us parents can become more realistic about what's going on in our lives. We can grow in the courage to face our problems and in the openness to receiving joy. We can also work on reversing the tendency to focus on the negative, on what we lack, so that equal time and attention is given to the positive—what we have. As we do this, we will notice that our sense of gratitude begins to increase. Gratitude is good for us; it makes us feel good physically, mentally, and spiritually. Because gratitude sensitizes us to moments of joy, we are less likely to miss them when we are grateful than

▼

What makes us feel good about ourselves? Knowing we are loved and hearing it again and again with lots of hugs and affection.

when we are focusing on the negatives. It is also natural to praise God when we are grateful. Praising God is also good for us physically, mentally, and spiritually.

In being realistic about our parenthood we need also to take seriously the question Job asked when all his troubles began. When his wife in her discouragement said to him, "Do you still persist in your integrity? Curse God and die," Job responded by asking, "Shall we receive the good at the hand of God, and not receive the bad?" (Job 2:9-10). While we may not put it in the same words because there are complex questions about whether God sends evil or whether God uses it when it comes, basically what Job is saying is that if joys and pains are part of life in this world, why should we be spared the pains?

A few days after Sally's death, a friend called to comfort us. When I (Bill) said something like, "Why did this happen to us?", he responded immediately, "Why not?" I resented this. The fact that I still remember it after many years shows how emotionally I received it. I still believe that he was being insensitive at that moment of excruciating pain, yet I realize he had a point. Because these things happen, who am I to think that they shouldn't happen to me?

So in our parental pains, whatever they are, who are we to think we should be spared them? This was the risk we took in becoming parents. God has not promised that we would be spared what so often is the common lot of humanity. God also is pained by our pains. God has compassion in our struggles with events in our life. What God has promised us is to be with us in our pains and to use them for our personal growth and for the development of our relationships. God has promised to use both joys and pains in clearing and deepening the communication with our families. And God will do this as we parents open ourselves to the wider possibilities, present in every moment, that are revealed to us through the vision of faith.

▼

Things to Talk About and Do

1.   How do you feel about the fact that parenthood is forever, that no matter how old your children become you will still be parents?

2.   Think of your life together as a family. Write about some of the major joys and pains you have experienced and how God was with you during those times.

Joys

Pains

3.   When you have experienced losses, large or small, who or what helped you through the grieving time?